"Katariina Rosenblatt recounts her chi what no human being should ever be e. courage to embrace the pain after so many years and to use it toward healing domestic minor sex trafficking survivors as well as toward raising awareness about this horrendous problem in our communities."

—Dr. Roza Pati, professor of law and executive director,
graduate program in intercultural human rights,
St. Thomas University School of Law;
director, Human Trafficking Academy;
member, Pontifical Council for Justice and Peace, The Vatican

"Katariina Rosenblatt is one of a multitude of children who have been and are being trafficked in our backyards every day. Her story is compelling and difficult to put down and at times may seem unbelievable, but the heinous things she endured are typical of the atrocity of trafficking that happens even in our country. Katariina's story is riveting, her healing is miraculous, and her courage to grasp her own recovery and help others is indescribable. Her faith is evident and elicits faith in the reader about God's love and commitment to us, even when we are not on the 'right' path. She is a living testimony of the love of God. I highly recommend *Stolen*. Katariina's story is a shining example of one who has come out of darkness and steps into that darkness to rescue others and bring them light and love."

—Nita Belles, author of *In Our Backyard*;
founder and director of In Our Backyard 365;
Central Oregon regional director of
Oregonians against Trafficking Humans

"Rosenblatt invites us to join her in a harrowing journey as a vulnerable and abused child who was intentionally groomed and then sexually exploited. Her book is a disturbing portrayal of the situations that put our children at risk and enable traffickers to exploit their vulnerability. Katariina escaped a life of abuse and has gone on to complete graduate training in law, receive a PhD, and found a faith-based organization to assist young women who are trapped in a world she experienced firsthand. She now dedicates her life to intervention, advocacy, and serving those at risk of exploitation. Her book offers hope and concrete guidance for action. Katariina's life story challenges us to deeper vigilance, prayer, compassion, and courage on behalf of children and other vulnerable people in our society."

—**Bill Prevette, PhD**, research professor
at Oxford Centre for Mission Studies, and
Ky Prevette, spiritual director, OCMS

"In *Stolen*, Kat clearly articulates details about something that most of us find hard to conceive. She shines light, both through her words and her faith, upon an industry that thrives in darkness. I would recommend this book to all parents no matter how secure they are in the belief that their children are immune to this crime. As frightening as it is to admit, they're not immune at all. And aside from helping readers understand better ways to protect their own children, *Stolen* can open discussions about opportunities for cleansing our communities of this corrosive industry. I would also recommend this book for teenagers because parents can't always be there to protect their children. Being able to learn from Kat's mistakes and identify the techniques of traffickers should help children steer clear of danger. It's a very important read."

—**Robert J. Benz**, founder and executive vice president,
Frederick Douglass Family Initiatives

STOLEN

THE TRUE STORY
OF A SEX TRAFFICKING SURVIVOR

KATARIINA ROSENBLATT, PHD
with CECIL MURPHEY

Revell

a division of Baker Publishing Group
Grand Rapids, Michigan

© 2014 by Katariina Rosenblatt and Cecil Murphey

Published by Revell
a division of Baker Publishing Group
P.O. Box 6287, Grand Rapids, MI 49516-6287
www.revellbooks.com

Printed in the United States of America

Library of Congress Cataloging-in-Publication Data
Rosenblatt, Katariina.
    Stolen : the true story of a sex trafficking survivor / Katariina Rosenblatt, PhD ; with Cecil Murphey.
        pages cm
    ISBN 978-0-8007-2345-3 (pbk.)
    1. Rosenblatt, Katariina. 2. Human trafficking—United States. 3. Prostitution—United States. 4. Child prostitution—United States. 5. Prostitutes—Rehabilitation—United States 6. Church work with prostitutes—United States. 7. Church work with abused women—United States. I. Murphey, Cecil. II. Title.
HQ281.R76 2014
306.74092—dc23   2014019042

Scripture quotations are from the Holy Bible, New International Version®. NIV®. Copyright © 1973, 1978, 1984, 2011 by Biblica, Inc.™ Used by permission of Zondervan. All rights reserved worldwide. www.zondervan.com

To protect the privacy of individuals who are still living, some names and details have been changed. The following is the author's personal recollection of the events of her life.

In keeping with biblical principles of creation stewardship, Baker Publishing Group advocates the responsible use of our natural resources. As a member of the Green Press Initiative, our company uses recycled paper when possible. The text paper of this book is composed in part of post-consumer waste.

15   16   17   18   19   20   8   7   6   5   4   3

Dedicated to all survivors
of abuse and sex trafficking.
May God fill you with hope
and set you free forever.

Contents

1. Why Was I a Victim of Human Trafficking?   11

2. My New Friend   17

3. "You Can Call Me Daddy"   27

4. The Bridal Game   37

5. "You Have to Make It Right"   43

6. Left to Die   53

7. My Vulnerability   59

8. Enduring Rage   69

9. From Bullying to Cocaine   77

10. Another Escape   89

11. Enslaved . . . Again   101

12. Unsuspected Predators   107

13. Fearing Paco   111

14. Almost Busted   125

15. From Clubs to Gangs   131

16. A Modeling Career   135

17. Wedded Bliss?   145

18. Learning about Boundaries   155

19. Lessons from Law School   161

20. Making the Break   169

21. Living Alone   175

22. My Emancipation Proclamation   183

23. Changed   191

24. Rescue Ministry   195

25. Survivor Stories   205

26. Setting the Captives Free   217

About There Is H.O.P.E For Me, Inc.   227

Acknowledgments   231

1

Why Was I a Victim of Human Trafficking?

"Sex trafficking doesn't happen here," people often say, especially those from small towns. If it doesn't happen where they live, they're not personally affected. "It's a terrible thing," they admit, but it's also removed from them.

Or so they want to believe. And yet, sex trafficking happens everywhere, and no city or small town is immune. It happens to victim-prone children. For me it occurred in Miami, but it could have happened to any girl or boy in Cub Run, Kentucky, or Cedar Falls, Iowa.

My cowriter, Cecil Murphey, wasn't caught in human trafficking—but even in Iowa where he grew up, he easily could have been lured into the sex trade. He had many of the same problems and conflicts as I did.

He also fit the profile. Every story is different; each victim and survivor has a distinctive experience, but most of us can be profiled easily enough. And it's not a gender issue. The problems and needs of me (a female) and Cec (a male) weren't much different. Our dissimilarities revolve around what happened *after* our early molestation.

I tell a little of Cec's history because too many people assume that in human or sex trafficking, predators want only girls. That's not true. In my organization (There Is H.O.P.E. For Me, Inc.) I have seen firsthand that at least one-third of sex slaves are boys.

Who are we? Why us?

We who were victimized didn't know healthy ways to cope with others. Usually, we were the loners, the outcasts, the shy, the overweight, or the smaller kids. Because we were needy children, perpetrators sensed that vulnerability. Most of us didn't meet some evil person lurking in the park, and we weren't accosted by a stranger on a dark street.

If those who lured us were strangers, they groomed us by winning our trust before they took advantage of our vulnerability. The point is that we knew our perpetrators and they taught us to trust them.

As you'll read in this book, my horrific childhood made me an excellent candidate. A woman named Mary groomed me—and *grooming* is the correct word. It means the perpetrator won my trust, showered me with attention, and made me feel important and special. That misplaced trust lured me into sex trafficking.

Why did Mary's methods work? Like other victims, I

didn't feel I had anyone who understood or cared. I felt useless and worthless. When my new friend Mary asked questions, listened to my answers, and made promises, she implied we would be friends forever. I received the attention I yearned for.

Although every child needs to be loved, the entrapment is more than just expressing affection (even though it's false affection). All children deserve to know they're loved and that they're special to their parents. It's not only whether they *are* loved but also whether they *believe* they are loved. That knowledge makes the difference.

Even though I always knew my mother loved me, she was a victim of my father's physical and verbal abuse. To make it worse, her submission to him was the only role model I had.

It's easy enough to say that we victims fit the profile of kids who had little self-esteem, although that's true. The label means we didn't feel we were worth much or that anyone cared about us. (Remember, it's how we assess the situation and not the reality.) If we don't feel loved, we have a built-in human need to seek affection and attention. That's how our victimization happens.

Several times I contemplated suicide. Another common theme is that most of us didn't learn from our families how to set boundaries or to take control of our lives. As you read my story, you'll realize that my father destroyed my boundaries, and so did those with whom I associated. Before I was out of my teens, I believed that females were inferior to males and deserved mistreatment. Why wouldn't I have been a good candidate for trafficking?

That's who we were as children: needy, insecure, anxious, lonely, and vulnerable. Without the maturity to make adult decisions, we didn't always know what was right or wrong. Instead, we felt something was wrong *with us* and that we were inferior to other children.

With that background, we wanted to believe our perpetrators' words and promises. When they flattered us, we believed them because we yearned to hear such words.

If you ask us, "How could you allow the abuse to occur?" we don't know how to respond. None of us wanted to be sexually assaulted; we never asked to be victimized. Who wants to be a sex slave? We wanted to feel worthwhile.

Our predators lied to and manipulated us. Worse, we believed their lies. We *needed* to believe someone—anyone—cared about us.

Because of my experience and my working directly with American children who have been victims of sex trafficking, I refer to the vulnerability factors that lead to recruitment of American children into sexual slavery.

Here are the most significant:

- abuse within the home, which normalizes that type of maltreatment
- economic disadvantages, such as coming from a single-parent home
- exposure to drugs and alcohol in the home, which makes that lifestyle seem normal
- seeking a father figure to fill a "daddy hole"

Opportunists are out there seeking to exploit genuine needs

for love and affection as well as basic needs such as food, clothing, and shelter.

This book is about my experiences. Despite the terrible things that happened, I am one of the lucky ones. I'm a grateful survivor and want to be the voice for those who cannot or will not ever be able to speak for themselves.

Most human trafficking victims don't survive. By the time they reach their twenties, they are worthless to the human trafficking trade. They're either drug-addicted or they become recruiters themselves. Many die from disease, drug overdose, or murder. Sometimes they see that their only way out is through suicide. In many cases, once children are recruited, their families don't hear from them again.

My story recounts a different ending. I survived because I escaped—more than once. The fact that I experienced human trafficking on more than one occasion is a phenomenon that should never have occurred. But once we're hooked into the lifestyle, it takes a great deal of courage and persistence to get out for good. God's pursuing love finally gave me that courage and enabled me to leave and to keep resisting the temptation to go back to slavery.

Many children never escape the life of commercial sexual exploitation. When their traffickers are finished with them, or if they run away, most of them—as I have seen many times— become deeply involved in the adult entertainment industry as a way of life. Because of the abuse and exploitation, that's the only lifestyle they have known since childhood.

Just escaping isn't enough, which is a major reason for this book. It took me years to believe in myself and to realize that God wanted me to have a good life that I deserved.

Since I escaped and grew in my faith, God has enabled me

to use my painful experiences to reach out to those young girls and boys who remain trapped in a life of sex trafficking.

Two things I need to point out:

First, I've tried to tell my story as honestly as I can, and obviously sometimes I can say only how I perceived someone else's actions.

Second, the stories about the girls and the traffickers in this book are true. For the safety of the girls, I have changed their names. Their lives may still be in danger, and I want to do everything I can to protect them.

After reading this book, I hope you'll see the need to help people like me and organizations like There Is H.O.P.E. For Me, Inc. that seek to rescue enslaved children and teens.

2

My New Friend

nother boring day," I said as I lingered at the shallow end of the pool. I had few friends and didn't know any kids to play with. We were living temporarily in the Dynasty, what I'd call a middle-class hotel in Miami Beach. It was moderately priced for the average American family to stay for a few nights, although a number of residents lived there permanently.

I wondered how long we'd stay. While I was growing up, my mother, brother, and I often moved. As a lonely, insecure, barely teenaged girl, I spent the summer days by the pool. I had nothing else to do except watch television.

I had already experienced sexual, physical, and verbal abuse, although I wasn't aware that it was abnormal. I struggled with feelings of low self-worth. Each morning, Mom left early for work because she had to take two buses to get to her job.

Since I had nothing to do and no responsibilities, every day was another day with no one to play with or talk to. I had cried so many times, it seemed I had no tears left.

A few hotel guests came to the pool, but none of them stayed long. Within a day or two they went back to Ohio or Maine.

One morning I was standing in the water at the edge of the pool. I closed my eyes, wishing the day were over. It was the same way I had felt the day before and the day before that.

"Hello there," a young woman said. I opened my eyes and stared at the smiling face of a beautiful blonde-haired woman with blue eyes. Thin and pretty, she looked like everything I wished I could be. She wore a red bikini and had the perfect figure for it.

"Hi," I said, surprised that she would talk to me.

"I saw you here by yourself," she said, "and you seemed sad and alone. I thought I would keep you company."

I mumbled something and she smiled again.

"Is it all right if we sit down and talk?"

I nodded, too excited to know how to respond. *She wants to talk to me. Maybe she wants to be my friend.*

"You must be lonely." Before I answered, she said, "My name is Mary, and I'm nineteen." She held out her hand. "What's your name?"

"Katariina, but everyone calls me Kat." I shook her soft hand and inhaled the sweet perfume she wore.

"Katariina is a nice name. How old are you?"

"Thirteen."

"Where's your family?" Her voice was warm and she continued to smile as she looked at me. Mary bent forward as she spoke, and I sensed she really wanted to get to know me.

18

"My mother's at work and—well, my dad doesn't live with us right now." I shrugged.

I got out of the pool, dried off, and stood in front of her, engulfed in my own thoughts, wallowing in self-pity, discontent, and loneliness (my usual thinking pattern).

Immediately I liked her. *She's so beautiful and confident. She's everything I would like to be.*

I still couldn't believe that she liked me, and I didn't think she had any flaws or could understand or imagine the rough childhood I had experienced.

Even in that first meeting, I yearned to be exactly like her. Mary had intense, bright-blue eyes that made me feel as though she could see right through to my heart. I began to feel she was the older sister I never had.

Mary smiled at me again, as if to say, "I understand, and I'm sorry." Within those first minutes, Mary gave me hope and offered me friendship and support. No one had ever treated me that way. I was bullied both inside and outside of my home; I had never had anyone stand up for me.

Looking back, I now know she chose me even before she talked to me. I'm sure she spotted the longing in my eyes and the loneliness that I projected out of my hurts and agony. As I would learn later, predators watch their victims before they target them. They especially seek lonely and abused children who display their vulnerability by the way they walk, their clothes, their general demeanor, or the helplessness in their eyes. Predators sense the children's lack of family support and their susceptibility. Only later could I see that my own identity was fragile and distorted. Then I would realize Mary had chosen me because she knew I was vulnerable and lonely.

For perhaps an hour, Mary sat on a lounge chair next to

me and we talked. It didn't take long for her to win my trust. She asked the right questions and focused on my eyes as I answered. No one had ever listened to me so intently before.

She told me almost nothing about herself, which I didn't think about until weeks later. Her questions expressed interest in me, something no one had ever done. Even at school, no one paid attention to me. I was tall for my age, slightly overweight, and I constantly sought approval from adults and older kids. But that approval rarely came. Even when it did, the longing in my soul was so desperate, the acceptance was never enough.

As I stared at Mary, I kept wishing I looked like her. She seemed sophisticated, the type who could stand up for herself—nothing like me. I could tell she'd had a rough upbringing from her references to parents and those in authority. And like any naïve teenage girl, I opened up quickly and talked freely, deliriously happy to have someone older who would listen and care about my thoughts and feelings.

Mary related to my tales of abuse (although I didn't know that word) with comments such as, "Your dad hurt you, huh? I know what you mean. My dad did that too when I was growing up. That's why I ran away."

After I told her a little more, she said, "You shouldn't be mistreated like that. It wasn't fair what happened to you. You should have had somebody there to defend you and protect you. If I were your sister, if I had been there, I would have done that for you."

It wasn't only her words, but the tender sound of her voice had exactly the right tone. I'd never met anyone whose hurts and wounds seemed to mirror my own. Of course, I didn't realize it at the time, but she listened to my words and used them to describe herself so she'd appear to be like me. So I would relate to her.

As would be obvious later, I was being groomed for the life of sex trafficking.

As a naïve thirteen-year-old, I found it easy to like Mary. Why *wouldn't* I like her? She showed interest in an affection-starved girl. She kept talking to me. The attention Mary gave me made me feel special. *Here's someone who cares about my feelings.*

Before the end of our first meeting at the pool, I was convinced that Mary was someone who would stand up for me and love me. In her presence, I felt good—better than I had in a long time. I had come back to life again because someone liked me and cared for me. No longer was I alone. I had a true friend, someone to confide in, who would comfort me when I needed it.

My new friend told me about herself—or at least what she thought I wanted to know—to gain my trust. But when I asked a direct question, she seemed to avoid it and acted as if she was more interested in listening to me. Instead of being hurt by her indirectness, I thought she was mature and confident, able to keep things to herself. That made me want to be like her even more.

Instead of talking about herself the way most people did, she plied me with questions about what I thought and how I felt. Instead of noticing that I might be in danger, I thought it was sincere care and concern for my well-being. With her constant caring reactions to my hurts, we grew closer and closer each day, developing a strong bond and relationship.

No one else in my life seemed to have time for me. My mom was working many, many hours; my dad was abusive;

and my older brother didn't want me hanging around. With Mary, however, I felt loved, wanted, and valued.

"What's your home life like?" Mary asked, and didn't look away from me. No one had ever paid so much attention to me. "Tell me about your mother. What's the relationship like with your dad?" She gained insight into all the hurts of my heart and found that my biggest wounds stemmed from what I now call a "daddy hole."

Each day as Mary listened, I poured out my sad responses, and she often replied with simple statements such as, "I'm sorry to hear that." Two or three times she patted my arm. It felt wonderful—I suppose that any type of kindness, even the slightest touch, was better to a lonely soul than being ignored or abused. Her older, sisterly affection made me feel valued, safe, and loved. Right from that first meeting, I trusted her.

She wants to know everything about my terrible life. Mary is my friend.

I told her things I hadn't ever told anyone else. Although my parents were divorced, Mom worked for my father, so he was still a part of our lives. He came to see us whenever he wanted. His language and behavior were abusive. Even though he earned good money, I rarely received anything from him unless I worked for it. I had already learned that I had to earn love in order to receive it. Mary was different, and when I was with her it was easy to forget about my pain and loneliness.

After that first morning, my summer days became wonderful and exciting. Every morning I hurried out to the pool, waiting eagerly until Mary showed up. And she came. Every morning. On the second or third day, she said, "I'm going to help you lose weight."

I wasn't fat, but I was overweight. I was also at the age when I noticed boys and wanted them to like me. But as someone who was inexperienced with the opposite sex, I knew I needed her help to gain their attention.

"We'll go for walks at night," Mary said. "I'll show you fun exercises and you'll lose weight."

That kind of talk pushed me to let down my guard. For the first time in my life, I was happy and contented. To be known and to know someone intimately as a friend and as a sister profoundly impacted me. I felt valued and worth something, and my self-esteem grew. Before long, she became my only priority. Whenever she said, "Let's go," I didn't hesitate to leave. Mary had chosen me as her friend. She could have befriended any girl, but she picked *me*.

She chose me.

I kept reminding myself that Mary could have selected hundreds of other girls to befriend. But she selected me and offered herself to me. I was too naïve to suspect her motives. She offered her friendship and I didn't have to do anything to earn it.

At least twenty-five years would pass before I would understand what it truly means to be chosen—to be chosen out of true love, not for evil exploitation.

There's one important element I want to inject here, because God began to play an important role in my life, even though it would take years for my life to change.

We didn't have much religion in our home, although my mother took me to whatever church was close by. In my memory, those churches were mostly filled with old people, and I was bored. Nothing made an impact on me. But when I was six years old, several youth members of a nearby Baptist church picked up my brother and me for their summer camp. It was a wonderful time away from home. Although I didn't remember the lessons, I felt the people were loving and sincere. I think they genuinely cared for us. That was my first memory of a real church experience.

My mother must have been searching for God in her life. Whenever a big-name evangelist came to Miami-Dade or Broward County, Mom wanted to attend the meetings. Because she didn't drive, she had to beg Dad to take us. He usually did—and always seemed angry and put out by the inconvenience.

I heard several famous evangelists such as Oral Roberts and Jesse DuPlantis. The one I most remember, however, and the man who changed my life, was Billy Graham. In 1985, he came to our area and held meetings in Fort Lauderdale.

My mother again begged Dad to take us; he agreed, although he wasn't happy about it. My brother didn't want to go, so there were only the three of us—Mom and Dad in front and me in the backseat. Dad yelled at Mom most of the way. By then, their yelling at each other had become such a normal part of my childhood that I paid little attention to the words.

Dad went inside with us but insisted we sit in the uppermost seats in the stands. "If I have to sit through this, that's where we're going." Obediently, we followed him. Throughout the entire evening, he didn't sing with us and I don't think he said a single word.

Billy Graham talked about "everlasting life, deep peace, and a joyful future," and I remember that statement and the words made sense, even to my young heart. As he spoke, I felt what I could only describe as a tug at my heart.

At the end of his message, Dr. Graham gave what I later learned was an altar call, in which he urged people to come forward and surrender their lives to Jesus Christ.

I turned to my mother. "I want that—I want what he's talking about."

I didn't understand what most of the words meant, but I grasped the love and sincerity coming from that man, and I would never forget it. What he offered was better than what my home life was like—getting pushed around, beaten up, and enduring Dad's verbal, mental, emotional, physical, and even sexual abuse.

I don't know if Mom gave me permission or if I just told her and started down the aisle. It seemed a long, long way to go, but I didn't care. I wanted what Mr. Graham promised.

Just as I got to the front, the evangelist turned and faced me. As a child of twelve, I was sure he was speaking only to me when he pointed his long index finger toward me. "Remember this: God will never leave you or forsake you."

I cried when I heard those words.

Through Billy Graham, the message became embedded in my heart. Even now, after all these years, I can close my eyes and see the evangelist standing with his left hand on a black Bible and the index finger of his right hand pointing at me. "Remember this: God will never leave you or forsake you."

———— ☼ ————

A woman laid her hand on my shoulder and talked to me about what it meant to become a Christian. I remember little of what she said because I kept thinking of those powerful words from the evangelist. She prayed with me and talked to my mom for a while.

Mom didn't pray to receive Jesus Christ at that time. She went forward and was interested and wanted to learn about God. But she had grown up in the Lutheran church in Finland, which didn't have calls for salvation. From the time I was little, she often told me about Jesus. Eventually, Mom became a believer, but only after seeing the life transformation that would occur in her daughter after years of tumultuous teen trauma.

That night, however, something happened in my life, and I felt happy and full of peace. We went back to where my dad was sitting in a row all by himself. He was impatient to leave, which was no surprise. Mom didn't say anything but she seemed unusually quiet.

When I walked out of the meeting, I had no way to know what was ahead for me. Years would pass before I was able to live the kind of life that Billy Graham talked about and experience the blessings a life of obedience would bring. During the next twenty years, my life was filled with fear, chaos, humiliation, and shame. And yet, even in the worst moments, I could still hear those words: "Remember this: God will never leave you or forsake you."

Those words would later prove to be true, living, and active, even in the midst of being bought and sold by human traffickers.

Billy Graham pointing his finger at me and speaking the healing words of God was something that never left me. When he said "everlasting life, deep peace, and a joyful future," those statements made sense in my heart.

Even though Mom seemed more at peace, Dad's violence and anger didn't go away or even lessen.

3

"You Can Call Me Daddy"

Not only did Mary promise to help me and to become my friend, but she kept her word about everything she promised. Besides being my daily companion, Mary helped me lose weight. She taught me how to dress better and to look sexy around boys; she built up my self-esteem so that when—and only when—I was around her, I felt good about myself.

In a world where I'd been able to count on nobody but myself, Mary was reliable. And she won over my mother because she would say to her, "I'm going to take Kat to . . . What time do you want her back?"

No matter what time my mother set, Mary always had me back on time and usually a little early.

We walked everywhere in the area. "This will help you lose weight," she said. "We'll walk a lot every day."

I especially remember the day we stopped in the middle of a bridge near our hotel. "I'm your friend, Kat."

"I know, and I love you."

"I'll always be your friend." She touched my arm. "You can talk to me about anything."

I believed her—that was part of the grooming process, for me to trust her without questioning.

I couldn't get used to the idea that Mary had chosen me to be her friend and wanted to spend time—a lot of time—with me and only me.

However, that day something odd happened while we were walking through a residential area. She pointed to a ranch-style house, which was much like the others in that area. "That's where my boyfriend, John, lives."

She explained that he was *one* of her boyfriends and that I would soon have boyfriends who loved me, just like she did. Before I could ask any questions, she grabbed my arm, and we crossed the street and stood in front of the man's house.

She cautioned me to be quiet as we walked right up to the window of his bedroom. He was a grown man, maybe forty years old, stretched out on the bed sleeping. He was naked.

"Oh—he's—he's not wearing—"

"That's just the way John likes to sleep," she said. "I know you're not used to seeing naked men, but it's all right."

As we moved away, she said, "I love him. And one day we'll be together."

"If he's your boyfriend and you love each other, why can't you be together?"

"Yes, we are in love." Mary smiled before she added, "and one day you'll have boyfriends like John."

I listened as she told me how much she loved him. Then she told me some of the sexual things they did together.

"But if he's your boyfriend, why aren't you married?"

"His mother. She doesn't approve of our being together."

Mary continued to talk, but something bothered me—it just didn't feel right. I wondered why his mother wouldn't approve. "Why doesn't she like you? I think you're wonderful, and if you're in love, you *should* be together." To my thirteen-year-old mind, it seemed only natural that if you love someone you should be married. I felt angry that my special friend couldn't be with her true love.

Mary must have seen I was upset because she hugged me and said, "It's all right. It will work out for us. But for tonight, I'm going over there to give him pleasure."

"What does that mean?"

Mary explained that she would sneak into his house and they would do things in his bed. I still didn't understand—it sounded too grown-up for me.

We started walking and soon the mood turned light again, and I stopped thinking about the naked man on the bed. Mary walked me back to the hotel. "I'm going to leave you and go back to his house alone," she said, "and take care of my man."

Mary and I went out during the daytime while Mom was at work.

My mom was extremely naïve; however, she did ask questions, such as "Where are you going? What are you going to do? When will you be back?" At first, Mom was skeptical. She reminded me that Mary was grown and I was a child—and like any thirteen-year-old girl, I resented being called a child.

Around Mary, I felt grown-up. She let me wear her shoes, borrow her things, and that made me feel as if I were beginning to look and act like her, my role model, idol, and hero.

Soon after our friendship began, Mary took me down to the pool. She pointed toward one of the most handsome men I'd ever seen. "I work for him," she said, although she didn't say anything more about her job.

I was so focused on his kindness toward his children and his beautiful blue eyes and good looks that I didn't think to ask what she did. The man was tall, blond, and broad-shouldered. He was in the pool, playing with his two little children. He threw them up in the air, caught them, and dropped them into the pool. As I watched, I wished I had a dad like him who thought spending time with me was important.

When Mary introduced us, he smiled, held out his hand, and said, "My name is Chet, but you can call me Daddy."

He introduced me to his three-year-old son, and the girl was a year younger. Even though my own dad was crazy and abusive, I knew all dads weren't like that. He was playing with his kids, so in my mind he was a good man. He turned away from us to play with the children again. I liked the casual way he related to his kids.

He's the kind of daddy I wish I had.

That particular morning I was hungry, and as often happened, Mom didn't have any money for snacks during the day. While Daddy was playing with his kids, I asked Mary if I could have a dollar to buy taco chips. Early in our friendship, she encouraged me to ask for money when I wanted a snack.

Instead of handing me a dollar as she'd always done, she said just loud enough for Chet to hear, "He'll give you anything you want." She nudged me toward him. "Just ask."

"Could I—could I have a dollar?" I asked him, reluctantly. Even though he was a stranger, he seemed like a nice, friendly man. Besides, my best friend told me I could trust him.

"Of course." He reached over to his wallet that was at the edge of the pool and pulled out a dollar bill. "Here," he said.

I reached for the money, but he held on to the dollar for a few seconds and smiled. Before he let go, he said, "But one day you'll owe me."

"What does that mean?"

"Don't worry, Kat. You'll know when that day comes," Daddy called and smiled again. "And I don't want you to say no." He winked and said, "You owe me now." Even though he seemed to be teasing, the words didn't sound quite right to me. Daddy turned back to his waiting kids and played with them again.

As Mary and I walked away, I asked, "What did he mean by that?"

"Stop worrying, he's just playing." Mary laughed, but the laugh sounded different than it usually did. Maybe a nervous laugh—I'm not sure. I was confused because I could tell he was serious. Perhaps that's why I never forgot his words.

Daddy must have seen the worried expression on my face, because he waved and smiled again at me, the way he did when he played with his children.

As I ate the chips, I didn't ask Mary again about what he meant, but something didn't feel right. *However*, I reminded myself, *I don't have to do anything I don't want to do*. My immature, thirteen-year-old mind couldn't imagine what he would want me to do anyway. It was only one dollar. How would he want me to pay that back?

31

Even though I didn't understand what he meant then, the day came when I would.

Mary was grooming me, of course, but I didn't realize what was happening. The process took about a month. By then, I had absolutely no doubt that Mary loved me and would do anything for me.

Most mornings we continued to meet at the pool. She sat beside me and we chatted about my family and what I wanted to do when I grew up.

One day she asked, "Do you like boys?"

I was a little embarrassed but admitted that I did, although I didn't talk about any boy in particular.

"What kind of boys do you like?"

We talked about several boys I knew, but I also told her I never got the attention of the boys I really liked.

"I'll help you with that," she said and patted my arm.

The next day she introduced me to a boy named Ralph who used to do flips at the pool to get the attention of the young girls in the hotel. Mary and I talked about him because the girls thought he was cute.

Ralph was handsome and muscular, and I thought he was probably Mary's age. He had a warm, disarming smile. Sometimes he looked at me and winked.

"Ralph likes you," Mary said the following day.

"He doesn't!" No older boy had ever liked me before, so her words stunned and excited me, but they also scared me a little.

"Yes, he does, and he wants to spend time with you." She smiled before she said softly, "Would you be interested? He says he wants to talk to you. Alone."

I hadn't been alone with boys before. I was intimidated. "What will he think of me? I probably don't know how to do the things he wants me to do. You know, the kinds of things you know how to do."

"There's nothing to worry about," she said. "He's a nice boy. And don't forget how many other girls would like to be alone with him. But he wants *you*."

Although flattered by her words, I hesitated. After Mary pressured me several times, I finally said yes.

"That's wonderful." Mary hugged me. "You'll like him. I'll talk to Ralph today and arrange for you to meet."

The next day, Mary and I walked up one floor and down the hallway. Ralph was waiting outside one of the rooms. An older Haitian maid, who worked at the hotel, stood in front of the door. Mary handed her money (I didn't see how much it was), and the woman turned and unlocked the door. Ralph gestured for me to go inside.

To my surprise, the room was dark and I could see nothing. Just then, the laughing voices of a boy and a girl made me know we weren't alone. As my eyes adjusted to the dark, I saw two double beds. Kids (probably teens) were in the far one. Their laughing and giggling made it seem they were having fun. They paid no attention to us.

Ralph winked at me and took my hand. Gently, he led me to the vacant bed and motioned for me to lie down. I obeyed him, but I felt uncomfortable. He sat on the edge of the bed and talked to me in a soft, quiet voice. "Have you ever been with anyone before?"

"No," I said. I knew what he meant, and I was scared. I could feel my body stiffen as he stroked my arm.

He leaned closer and I could smell alcohol on his breath.

"Everything is going to be all right," he said in a soothing voice. He stroked my hair and his hands slowly moved down my body.

I began to cry.

"Have you ever had sex before?"

"No! No!" I said, and my crying grew louder. I couldn't help myself and I became even more frightened.

Ralph was gentle, although I sensed he didn't really want to be in the room with me. "It's okay," he said, then took my hand and helped me out of the bed. He opened the door where Mary and the maid waited outside.

"She's a virgin," he said, and his voice sounded cold and indifferent.

Mary smiled, obviously pleased to hear those words. They talked softly, their backs to me so I couldn't hear.

But I was out of the room and that made me feel better. I was relieved because I didn't have to do anything.

At the time, I had no way of knowing that they wanted to make sure I was a virgin before they did anything else. Even though I didn't know it, in those days selling a virgin to a man was worth several hundred dollars. Mary wanted to make sure I was who I said I was. Apparently, my fear and crying convinced Ralph.

He waved good-bye and walked down the hall, away from us.

Mary put her arm around my shoulders. "It's all right, Kat." She smiled, and her voice sounded like she was still my friend. "Oh, there's one thing you can do for me." Her blue eyes focused on me and I felt warm and loved.

"Anything."

"I want us to play a game—a fun game. In this game, you're going to be the bride, and there is a man in the hotel who wants to be a daddy to you. And *you* are the only one he wants."

"Me?"

"Only you."

Once again, I felt *chosen*. I was extremely naïve and didn't even think about the difference between being a bride and his being my daddy. Mary had tapped into my great need for a kind, loving male figure in my life.

"It will be a lot of fun, I promise you. We'll do it tomorrow. And when we meet, I want you to wear a white dress. Do you own a white one?"

I nodded. "Well, sort of." I described it to her and said it was made of denim and didn't have much shape to it.

"That's fine. You'll have fun."

Seconds later, Mary's mood changed to fun-loving friend once again when she asked, "Hey, want to get something to eat?"

In retrospect and with maturity, I now understand what was going on. She wanted to make me feel secure again about being with her. As she had before, Mary laughed when I said something funny.

"I'm sorry for the terrible life you've had. I want to be your friend—and you can trust me."

I did trust her. Why wouldn't I? She liked me.

Mary acted sorry for what had happened with Ralph. She didn't apologize, but she kept telling me that everything was going to be all right and for me not to worry.

Mary talked enthusiastically about our new game. "Meet me in the stairwell tomorrow afternoon around five o'clock, and then we'll have fun." She could probably see the trust and vulnerability on my face. Just before she left me, however, she said, "But you can't tell your mom. All right?"

"Why not?"

"Because it's a special game and we wouldn't want to ruin the surprise for her when you come home with all of the new stuff you're going to get."

"But why can't I tell her?"

"Your mom won't understand, and it's a little complicated to explain," Mary said as she slipped her arm around my waist. "You can tell her you're going to be with me for the evening."

"Okay, as long as I can tell her later. Will that be all right?" I asked.

"Yes, that will be all right then."

I went back to the room and was excited about the game we were going to play. I was going to meet a man who wanted to be a father to me. It sounded wonderful because I would finally have a father—a man who would love me. Because he loved me, of course he would be nice to me, take me shopping, and I could do the things other kids got to do. I would be normal.

The next morning when Mom saw me getting dressed up, I told her I was going to spend the day with Mary.

"I hope you'll have fun together," were her last words to me.

We didn't have much money, and I had only the one white dress. Mom had bought it for me months earlier so I could look good when I went to a special event with my father.

After Mom left, I put on her blush and other makeup and fixed my hair with her curling iron. I wanted to look pretty for Mary's sake and to impress the nice daddy-man.

That morning I had no idea that the game could result in my mother never seeing me again.

4

The Bridal Game

Mary was waiting for me in the stairwell at five o'clock. I felt nervous and excited.

"The dress is perfect!" She looked me over, made me twirl around. She commented that my makeup and dress made me special. "You make such a beautiful bride."

"You really think so?"

Several times she told me how nice I looked—and I believed her. "You will have so much fun, I promise. Come on," she said, pulling me after her up the stairs to the second floor. We stopped at a room and Mary knocked.

A man with gray hair and a wrinkled face opened the door. "Please, come in," he said and smiled at me. He was heavy with a beer belly hanging out over his belt, and he wore only a pair of gray dress pants.

"Here's your girl," Mary said as we stepped inside and shut the door behind us. "She's ready for you."

"You are so lovely," he said. He smiled and asked me a few questions. He seemed nice enough, but something wasn't right. He stroked my hair and rubbed my shoulders. I wanted to believe that man cared for me. I desperately needed to know that I was loved and that he would be a daddy to me.

Although I can't explain, it didn't feel as if we were playing a game, and I wasn't sure what was happening. He touched my face, patted my shoulder, and his hand moved down to my neck. "So young. So pretty. So sweet."

Mary turned to the door, and just then a click made me know she had locked it. "I want you to meet Katariina," she told the man. "Kat, he's my friend."

"You are so pretty," he kept saying to me.

I smiled. Why wouldn't I? That was something my father had never told me. I was confused and a little scared, but I yearned to hear such words from a man.

And yet . . . why did he make me feel uncomfortable? Something about the way he looked at me and the way it felt when he touched me didn't feel right.

He walked over to the nightstand and motioned for me to sit next to him on the bed.

I didn't move.

"Would you like to sit next to me, honey?"

Chills went down my spine, and like the nice, polite girl my mom had always taught me to be, I said, "No, thank you, sir."

My voice felt shaky because I was scared. I stared at Mary. Until then I hadn't realized she was dressed for the beach and wore a blue cotton blouse over her bikini. *Why am I dressed up and she's not?*

"What's going to happen now?" I asked Mary. "Are you going to leave me?"

"No, I'm right here," she said, but she stayed near the door, as if guarding it from my going out or anyone coming in.

Not sure what to do, I knelt by the bed instead of lying down as I had done with Ralph. Without consciously doing so, I was kneeling in a prayer-like position, my eyes were closed, and I started asking God to help me. *What should I do? I'm scared and don't know what to do.*

Just then, the words Billy Graham had said at his crusade filled my mind: "Remember this: God will never leave you or forsake you." I pictured Mr. Graham standing there, pointing his right index finger at me, reassuring me that God loved me.

I looked up as Mary finished rolling a marijuana cigarette and put it on a tray. I looked at her inquisitively while she lit the joint and pretended to smoke it before she passed it to the man. Both of them pretended to smoke it.

Mary held it out to me. "Here, Kat, try it. It's good for you."

Because I could see that they weren't really smoking it, I knew something wasn't right. *Why are they trying to trick me?*

The old man on my left side and Mary on my right made it clear that she intended for me to stay in the room after I smoked it. She laid the joint on the tray. Once before I had tried marijuana with some rough kids and I hadn't liked it.

"It's all right," the old man kept saying in a quiet voice. "You don't have to be afraid." He lightly stroked my hair and my shoulders. "Don't be afraid. I won't hurt you."

I didn't take the pot, but I calmed down.

"How much will you pay for your girl?" Mary asked him. "She's ready for you."

"I'll pay five hundred."

I was for sale! I stared in bewilderment as they bargained for *me*.

"No, that's not enough," Mary said with a hard edge on her voice. "She's a virgin. I want five-fifty."

Instead of answering, he turned to me. "Are you a virgin?"

"I don't know," I said.

"Have you ever had sex with anyone?"

"No."

He looked at Mary, nodded, and said, "All right then. I'll pay five-fifty."

That's when I understood how much I was worth to them— five hundred fifty dollars.*

As they talked, I kept hearing Billy Graham's words inside my head. I sensed that smoking the pot would have been the end of my resistance. Although I hadn't seen it happen, I'd heard of kids who had smoked pot and gone limp like spaghetti. They weren't able to walk or do anything, and I didn't want that.

Silently and fervently I prayed, repeating the promise of God through Billy Graham.

Mary smiled as she held the joint out to me again.

I shook my head. "No, thank you."

"Take it!" Mary's voice no longer sounded friendly and kind.

I shook my head again.

"Take it! Now!" The man's voice was louder and demanding, but I wasn't going to give in. Finally, he looked at Mary and then back at me. "Would anybody miss you if you were gone?"

*As I learned later, that was the going rate for an American virgin girl.

"My mom would miss me," I said. "She's downstairs right now cooking dinner for me, and I need to go home soon."

"What's going on?" he shouted at Mary.

"Taste it!" Mary held the joint only inches from my mouth. Then she softened her voice again. "It's okay, Kat. It's good for you."

Only later, after I was truly trapped in sex trafficking, did I realize that she had probably laced the joint with something that would have made me totally compliant.

The man picked up the joint and again pretended he was smoking. "See! It's really good."

"No, thank you," I said once again. As I spoke, I felt a strange boldness that I hadn't known before. I didn't hear a voice, but inside my heart I kept hearing these words: *Don't take the pot.*

Mary and the old man tried to reason with me. He finally asked, "Would anybody be able to hear you if you screamed right now?"

"Yeah, my mom would hear me. I would scream really loud and she'd come looking for me." I stared right into his eyes with defiant boldness.

I was also scared and confused. *Mary is my friend. Why did she bring me to this man? What are they planning to do to me? Why is he asking me so many questions? Is he planning to kidnap me? Why would Mary do such a thing to me? He's a bad man—I know that now.* I could feel it in my heart, that yucky he's-a-stranger-and-I'm-in-danger feeling. *Doesn't Mary see that he's bad?*

I stood up, hands on my hips, and showed them I wasn't going to submit. *You're not going to get me. I'm a big girl so you'll have to tackle me.*

"Get out of here! Get out of here!" the man shouted. He grabbed my arm, unlocked the door, and pushed Mary and me into the hallway.

"Wait!" Mary yelled as he shoved her out of the room.

"Forget it, forget it. It's too dangerous. Besides, I've lost interest." He slammed the door behind us.

The lock clicked.

I never doubted God had rescued me from that terrible scene. And it wouldn't be the last time God had to intervene in my life.

5

"You Have to Make It Right"

can't believe you messed up like that!" Mary shouted at me. "I can't believe you did that! Now you're going to have to pay for it, and now I'm going to be in trouble with Chet."

I stared at her, unable to figure out what I had done wrong.

"I'm going to have to pay for the mess you made, and I'll be in so much trouble." The venom in her eyes shocked me because Mary had never spoken that way to me before. "It's all your fault!" She said those words several times and she sounded just like my dad.

I felt bad right then, asking myself, *What did I do? How had I messed up?* I couldn't understand what was going on. Mary had promised me that it would be fun, but it didn't feel like fun.

Because she had enticed me with her false friendship, I

started denying my feelings; her love and acceptance were more important. At that age, I was willing to do whatever she wanted to make it better. And as a survivor of abuse, I grew up believing that my own thoughts and feelings didn't matter and should be discounted.

"I won't mess up again," I said. "I promise. I'm sorry—"

"Okay then," she said. "I'll forgive you, but you have to make it right."

"Please, just tell me what to do. I'll do anything! I promise." The tears began falling and I couldn't stop them. It hurt so much that my best friend was angry because I had ruined things for her. "Just—just tell me what to do—"

"All right." Although her voice softened, it still had an edge to it. "I'm going to give you a chance, and you'd better not mess up again."

"I won't! I promise!"

"Just remember that you owe me. Now you have to make it up to me."

"I will, I'll make it up—"

"I'm in trouble. A lot of trouble." She didn't add "because of you," but I felt it.

I promised again, and just as I turned to walk away, she said in a strong, low voice, "I know where you live. I know who your mom is, so you'd better promise me that you're not going to tell anyone."

"Oh, I'm not going to tell," I said. "I promise. I'm sorry for the way I behaved."

Mary didn't have to say much to manipulate me. She had my friendship and she had my loyalty. I was scared, but I was more concerned that she wouldn't like me anymore. At age thirteen, I was still naïve. The money part confused me, and I wondered why Mary would want to sell me to that big-bellied man. I was afraid to ask.*

It didn't occur to me that the sex traffickers wouldn't let $550 slip past them.

Back in our room at the hotel, I didn't tell my mom what happened. But like any good mother, she could see my eyes were red from crying.

"What happened?" she asked. "I thought you were with Mary."

"I don't know, Mom. We were just playing a game."

"What happened?"

I shrugged as if to pass it off. "It's no big deal. I messed up. I don't know what I did wrong. Mary got mad at me—"

"I don't have a good feeling about that girl anymore," she said and embraced me. "I liked her at first, but lately—"

"No, it's my fault. I messed up."

"I don't want you to hang around her again." Her parenting instincts kicked in, even though she had no idea what had happened. It might have been too late, but at least she exerted authority. My mother's protective love enabled me to sleep that night.

Whatever dumb thing I had done, I was sure I could make it up to Mary.

By late afternoon the next day, Mary hadn't come, but other kids did. I'd met several of them and knew they were

---

*Mary had probably been recruited as a young girl and eventually became a recruiter, which is a common practice in child sex trafficking.

Mary and Chet's friends. We hadn't done anything together, but we knew each other.

One of them, Christina, was sixteen. I hadn't become friendly with her, because most of the time she was on drugs. When we tried to talk, she was usually stoned—like some zombie. That day when Christina came around, she seemed about half awake, which was more than she usually was. "I heard you messed up."

"Yeah, I guess I did."

"You messed up with Mary. Big time."

After I apologized—again—to her about my behavior, Christina said, "You have to make it up to Mary. You know that, don't you?"

"I know," I said, even though I had no idea what I was supposed to do.

"Get dressed. Come with me if you want to make it up to Mary. Right now! I'm going to take you out for some fun. A party, you know. You'll have a good time."

"Okay."

"It'll be fun, I promise you. Mary said you have to go with me if you want to make it better."

"I'm not allowed to hang around her anymore, so I can't go."

"Oh, but you have to make it up to her. You know, because if not, you can't show your face around here. And no one will like you. Just tell your mom you're with me. It will be okay if you tell her that. I promise you, we'll have a lot of fun. We'll have you home before you know it."

"Okay, I guess so."

"See, you're still a little girl and that's why you messed up," she said. "We want to help you so you won't do it again. You need to learn a few things. Like a big girl."

"What do I have to do?"

"Get dressed and I'll tell you. Put on something nice. Just tell your mother that you're with me and you won't be gone long."

I hurried inside and told my mom I was going to hang out for a little while with Christina, who was closer to my age. "She's a nice girl who lives around here," I said, even though I didn't know where Christina lived and I didn't know her very well.

"Is Mary going to be there?"

"Oh no, definitely not."

"All right," Mom said.

I didn't mention that Christina was sixteen years old, that she was on drugs, or that she was a friend of Mary's.

I believed we would be having fun like grown-ups or big girls, because that's the way Christina made it sound. If I went with her, she promised she'd fix everything and make it up to Mary for whatever happened in the hotel room that had caused her to be mad at me.

I got dressed in my best dress and I wore my black pumps—my big-girl shoes with mini heels. I looked like I was going out to dinner or somewhere fancy.

I came out of the hotel, ready for our fun adventure, and Christina was waiting. She greeted me and said, "We're going to go in a car."

"Oh no, I can't go anywhere in a car." I was afraid to go and just as afraid to say no to Christina.

"If you want to make things right, come with me and I'll fix things." She pushed away any objections and kept assuring me that everything would be fine. "And we'll have you back home in less than an hour." Christina opened the door.

"I—I don't know about this—"

"If you want to make it right with Mary, you'd better come with us."

"I don't want to go in the car."

"Just get in the car!" the driver said. "Now!"

"Either do this," Christina said, "or you're going to be in even more trouble with Mary."

"I guess I have to go," I said to myself. I got into the back-seat of a Honda Civic. There was a male driver I didn't know. Christina may have told me his name, but I wasn't listening. Something about getting into that car didn't feel right, but I didn't know what it was or how to refuse.

I stared at the driver, who was at least eighteen years old. I didn't like his voice or the way he stared at me.

"Where are we going?"

"You'll find out," the driver said and laughed.

At first he drove around in circles. I know that because there's a bridge from Miami Beach to the mainland in North Miami Beach. We went under the bridge twice.

"Why are you guys driving around like this? Where are we going? We're going around in circles, and I'm feeling dizzy."

"I'm looking for the place for our party." He drove around another five minutes and asked if I recognized where we were.

"Yes," I told him.

That also seemed strange. Didn't they know where they were going? Why would they ask me such questions? He kept driving. Then he drove over the bridge and made several turns.

"I don't know where I am now," I said. It didn't occur to me that they were trying to disorient me so I couldn't find my way back.

Finally, Christina pointed to a convenience store up ahead and mumbled something. The driver pulled into the parking lot. I started to move, but Christina said, "He's going to get directions."

"Hey, Kat, do you like fruit drinks?" he asked as he started to get out.

"Yeah, sure I do."

"I'm going to buy wine coolers," he said, and this time his voice sounded friendly, sweet even. "Do you like wine coolers?"

"I don't know. I never drank any."

"I'll buy you one. You'll really like it."

He got out of the car, went inside, and brought back a four-pack of wine coolers. I thought that was all part of the package of doing big-girl stuff to make things right with Mary.

A few minutes later, he pulled into a vacant parking lot and stopped the car. He leaned back toward me with a wine cooler in his right hand and a small, round, white pill in his left. "Here. Take this pill and wash it down with the wine cooler."

"What kind of pill is it? I don't want to take a pill."

"If you don't take it," he said calmly and stared right at me, "you're not going home."

"What time is it?" I asked.

"Eight o'clock," Christina said.

"It's too late. I need to go home," I said. "I have a curfew, and Mom will be really mad if I'm late." I didn't have a curfew, but it was the only thing I could think to say. "I can't play this game anymore. I have to go home."

"You're not going home—not yet."

"I don't want—"

"You take this pill or you're never going home! And you'll never see your mom again!"

"I don't want to—"

"It's okay, Kat. There's nothing wrong with the pill," Christina said. "It'll make you feel better, that's all."

I shook my head.

"If you do this, it will show Mary that you really want to make it up to her."

Still I hesitated. "I do want to make it up to Mary."

Christina looked at the driver. "Do you think one is enough?"

"Yeah, she's just a kid. One will do the trick."

I didn't understand what they meant, but no matter what I said, I knew I'd have to swallow the pill, because they would force me if I didn't.

"Okay," I said and took the pill from his hand, washing it down with the wine cooler. "Now take me home, please."

"We'll wait a few minutes," the driver said.

I didn't say anything, but I wondered why we needed to wait.

After perhaps five minutes, the driver opened my door. "Get out!"

"Why? I don't know where I am and—"

"You're going to feel a little sleepy," Christina said, "but don't worry. If you get too sleepy, just lie down. We'll come back to get you."

The pill had begun to take effect, and I was disoriented. I saw them get out and wondered if we were at the place for the party. I think they did that only so I wouldn't be afraid to get out of the car. But as soon as I was outside the car and saw what a lonely, empty place it was, I said, "Are you going to leave me? How will I get home?"

"We'll be back."

Those were the last words I heard. They both got back inside the Civic, the door slammed shut, and the driver screeched away. As I watched, I tried to call out, but I couldn't. I became dizzy. Weak.

Unable to stand up, I collapsed on the gravel. As I lay on the rough ground, I thought, *I'm going to die here at age thirteen. I haven't even lived yet and this is how I'm going to die.*

6

Left to Die

I was dying. They had poisoned me, and I couldn't resist any longer.

I fell asleep.

"Get up and walk!" a strong voice shouted inside my head—and I've always believed that was God.

"I can't. I'm too tired."

"Get up and walk!" the voice shouted a second time.

"Help me, God. Please help me." Even though I can't explain it, I was able to stand up and I began to walk slowly. Stagger is probably more accurate. I was still wearing those little heels and kept thinking I was going to fall.

In front of me stood an abandoned building, and it was near the water. I was at an old marina. As I stumbled toward it, I saw a pay telephone attached to that rickety building.

I stumbled over to it, picked up the receiver, and heard a dial tone.*

No matter where I looked, everything was blurry and fuzzy. I felt disoriented. I was so nauseated and weak I could hardly hold on to the phone. I didn't have any money. Because I couldn't read any of the numbers, I fumbled around until I found zero and dialed.

"This is the operator. How may I help you?"

I tried to talk but the words weren't coming out very well.

Quietly but firmly she asked, "What's your name?"

"Don't know. Lost. Help me get home?"

"Where do you live?"

"I don't know. I don't live anywhere." My words were slurred and I probably wasn't making sense. "In a hotel."

"What's the name of the hotel?"

"Dynasty." I remembered that much.

"Hold on, sweetie. I know you're lost and you're drugged. I can hear it in your voice."

I must have said more, but I was so groggy I don't remember.

"Just stay on the line with me, okay?"

"Okay. Please . . . please . . . help me . . . get to my mom."

Although I don't know how long it took, someone at the desk of the Dynasty Hotel spoke to the operator. I could hear his voice and the hotel was small enough that he knew the permanent guests. Even though the man at the desk probably knew who I was, I couldn't say words that made sense.

"Who's your mother?"

"Ella . . . Ella . . ."

*Years later, when I told that part of my story, a man who worked for the phone company said, "You had a real miracle. When they abandon a building, we turn off the phone lines."

———— ☼ ————

"Yes, I know her," he said. He connected the operator with our room.

My mother was upset when the operator talked to her. "I told you not to go with that girl! I had a bad feeling about her. That Mary—this is her fault."

"No, no, Mom, it's not. It was the other kids. Please don't be mad at me because I went with them. I'm so sorry, Mom, I'm so sorry." I'm not sure I said all those words aloud—but I know I tried to say them. I was afraid that my mother would be mad at me. She said I slurred and paused between nearly every word.

The operator interrupted a few times in a quiet, kind voice. Finally, Mom calmed me down by saying repeatedly, "It's all right. It's all right." Then she asked, "Where are you?"

"I don't know . . . Don't know. Come . . . find me."

"Tell me where you are."

"I'm so sorry, Mom . . . I'm lost. I don't know, I came with them . . . a boy driving the car . . . made me take the white pill . . . and drink something. A wine cooler . . . I made a mistake." I was babbling, but I couldn't help myself.

"Listen carefully," the operator interrupted. "Look around you. Just tell us what you see."

While I was trying to describe things, Mom became hysterical and cried.

The calm voice of the operator blotted out Mom's wailing. "Take your time and look around you."

"Feel . . . like . . . I'm going to pass out . . ."

"We're going to help you," the operator said. She asked more questions. "What do you see near you?"

"Water."

"Do you see lights?"

"I see cars a ways off."

"So you're near a street. Do you hear cars?"

"Yes . . . and we went over a bridge . . . and I don't know . . . what happened. They made . . . made me . . . drink fruit drink . . . tasted funny."

Then I passed out.

My next conscious moment was looking into the worried face of my mother. She and a cab driver were lifting me up from the ground.

"Come back to me, Katariina, come back to me," Mom pleaded. "Wake up, please wake up."

I must have drifted in and out of consciousness. Mom got me back to the hotel. When I was clearheaded enough to understand her, she said I had given the operator enough information so Mom knew approximately where I was. With the help of the cab driver, they drove around until she spotted the dangling telephone. Then she saw me on the ground.

Mom didn't call the police, but she did call a doctor. She described everything she had learned about my being drugged.

When he asked to talk to me, I explained what I could. At first he thought they had given me speed, but he changed his mind when I described the size and shape of the white pill, the nausea, and my heart racing so fast I felt like it was going to explode.

He listened and probed with more questions. He was never positive what they had given me, but he said, "Whatever it was that they forced you to take, you have to stay awake. You can't go to sleep tonight. It sounds like what they gave you will kill you if you go to sleep."

"Kill me?"

"If you go to sleep, you'll never wake up."

I mumbled that I understood.

"I want you to walk around the hotel with your mother." Then he said to Mom, "Those people who did this to her are dangerous. She's thirteen. If it's what I think it was, that dose should have killed her." He paused before he said, "That was probably their intention. Drugs and alcohol don't mix."

After the phone call, Mom and I walked around the hotel until six o'clock the next morning. I expected her to be angry with me, and I deserved it. Instead, she was patient, loving, and kind. She rarely lost her temper, so when Mom had shouted at me on the phone, I now understood that it came out of her fear and anxiety.

She never told anyone what happened, but she did talk straight to me about Mary. "Now you know, don't you? Mary is *not* your friend."

"I don't think it was Mary. It was those other kids. They're the bad ones. Mary is the good one." I was not willing to give up the notion that Mary was my one true friend.

"Mary is not your friend! They're all part of the same group. She sent them to you."

I listened, not wanting to believe her, but I knew she was right.

"I want you to stay in this room," Mom said, "and you're not to leave while I figure out a new place for us to live. We can't stay here. Those people could try to kill you again."

What happened was my fault, and now we had to move. Mom didn't speak another critical word to me, but my shame increased. It proved to me once again that I was useless and always made bad choices.

I stayed in the room, but by the end of the day I was tired of doing nothing except watching TV. I sneaked out of the room and walked over to a nearby hotel. Just then, I spotted Mary. She was befriending a boy who looked like he was about ten years old. He was a white American boy who wore nothing but his swimming trunks and was barefooted. She leaned toward him, and from her bent-over position, I knew she was talking sweetly to him—the way she had talked to me.

Something inside me jerked, as if I instinctively knew that she would try to sell him too and use him to do the same thing she wanted me to do.

Mary must have sensed someone coming up behind her. She turned, stared at me, and her face turned ghostly white. She didn't say anything, but her expression said, "I thought you were dead."

"You wanted to kill me, didn't you?" I didn't give her a chance to say anything. "You're not my friend!" I turned around and ran back to the room.

By then, I was really scared. She wasn't my friend and I didn't know what she'd try to do to me if she got the chance. Now I knew the truth—and I cried as I said aloud, "Mary isn't my friend."

When Mom came home from work, I told her what happened.

"Don't ever leave the room again!"

I didn't leave the room until it was time for us to move out of that hotel. I was too afraid.

I thanked God for intervening and for sparing me. Repeatedly, I promised God I would never disobey my mom again.

And I meant it.

But that wasn't the end.

7

My Vulnerability

My childhood was terrible, and yet not any worse than that of many other victims of human trafficking. I had been chosen and groomed by Mary—which probably wasn't her real name.

Her name may have been false, but the method was real, and she used the techniques most human traffickers employ to steal and destroy the lives of ignored and sexually abused young people. Like me, those children and teens have little sense of self-worth. Why would they? They feel no one loves them and no one is looking out for them.

I was an ideal candidate. It didn't take much for Mary to notice my vulnerability and exploit me. She knew what she was doing, but I was blind to the multimillion-dollar industry of the sex trade that was going on behind the scenes.

Most people would think that after it happened once, I

would wise up to the lures and tricks of the trade. Actually, it made me more blind to the trafficking. We know that if a child is targeted once, they are more likely to be targeted again. As I had yet to learn, there develops an invisible chain that binds targeted children to their predators.

Three times I was seduced into a terrible lifestyle, and each time it was more serious. I took free cocaine and alcohol and endured the sexual abuse as a necessary evil. With no one standing up for me or stepping up to rescue me, I believed the lie that my lifestyle was acceptable.

That belief, along with the deadening effect of drugs and my continual yearning for love and affection, meant the sex was something I put up with. Eventually, I needed the drugs to get me through the days, weeks, and events. Because I lived in what I call a survival mode, I had no respect for myself. I was deadened to the life around me. At times, I felt I was some kind of pseudo-human.

By the age of fifteen, I thought my lifestyle was normal; it was how everybody like me lived. It didn't seem to matter, because I believed I deserved to be mistreated. Again, why not? The mistreatment had become an ingrained part of my lifestyle.

I hung around other kids who felt the way I did, and in each other we found acceptance. Being with others in the same situation helped us believe the way we were living was normal. Since we had no control over our environment and no one guided us in the right path, our behavior became familiar, and therefore it became easy for us to live in those compromising environments.

Despite that, something inside me knew it was wrong, but I had no one to point me in the right direction. Those who tried to tell me I was wrong or that I was doing terrible things with my life, I tuned out. They hadn't been there to stop my childhood sexual abuse, and I couldn't trust them.

Dad remained abusive to my mom, so I didn't respect her or her opinion. I thought if she couldn't protect herself or me, why should I listen to her? My mother came from Finland, and she had no awareness of such things as human trafficking. Where she lived, people trusted everyone and they didn't lock their doors at night. Several times I thought, *If I tell her, she'll freak out, overreact, and I don't know what she'll do.*

I kept silent.

Over time, I discovered that the love from my handlers was false, and eventually I was able to escape. Yet, even with the dehumanizing, perverse, and disgusting lifestyle, those in the trade know how to keep us trusting them and dependent on them. Long after we leave, the lure to return is there.

Some never move beyond that dependency.

I was one of the lucky ones. I survived the degradation of being a sexual commodity. Some say that fewer than 15 percent of human trafficking victims ever escape. Although I was fed cocaine regularly, I overcame my drug addiction. Unlike most victims, I didn't die before the age of twenty-five.

My story could have been like the stories of other victims I've known. Many of them are used up and dead by the time they reach the age of eighteen. Some survive to their twenties, but few live much longer. If they do get away, they rarely tell anybody, or they surrender to lives of prostitution or adult entertainment.

Most of those I hear from today stay addicted to drugs and sell their bodies to feed their habit—including children who have been sold by their parents to feed their own demanding, compulsive need for drugs. It becomes a horrible, vicious cycle of addiction and abuse from one generation to another.

Now I live to help other girls—and increasingly boys—to walk in freedom and find that they too can regain their self-respect and human dignity. Because I'm alive and free, I want to warn others about the dangers.

———— ☼ ————

Looking back, I can see that my childhood experiences made me vulnerable and set me up for the traffickers. Even before I was old enough to attend school, fear was an every-day occurrence. Mom and Dad argued a lot. Before long, it escalated into yelling at each other. One day, he threatened to kill her, and Mom's screaming grew louder. With tears in my eyes, I ran into the kitchen. Mom, wearing her bathing suit and barefooted, was trembling and trying to push him away.

He held a butcher knife a few inches from her throat.

"Don't kill Mommy! Daddy, please don't kill Mommy!"

He didn't kill her, of course, and I don't remember how it stopped. But after that, I worried that he might kill her. Not only did my father yell often, but sometimes he struck her with his fist. Other times he threatened to make *me* pay for our mistakes—even if I didn't know what mistakes we made.

———— ☼ ————

I was about five years old when my dad introduced me to inappropriate sexual contact. My parents were already divorced, and it was one of those many times when we lived with him because my mom depended on him and couldn't afford her own place.

That day Mom was working in the kitchen, and Dad was

in the bathroom with the door open. He called me. "Honey, come here. I want to show you something."

He stood in front of me, and his pants and underwear were at his knees. Because he hadn't done that before, I didn't know what to do.

"This is a privilege," he said quietly, and made it seem like I should be honored to look at his naked manhood.

I was afraid and began shaking.

"Here, touch me," he said.

Even at that age, I knew it was something that a little girl shouldn't do. Yet because he was my father, I did what he said. Even during my early teen years, he tried touching my breasts and his hands searched my body for "growth and maturity."

That first time, however, I called out to my mother, "Daddy asked me to touch his pee-pee! He made me touch his pee-pee!"

Mom rushed into the bathroom and yelled, "You dirty old man!"

By then he had turned away and pulled up his pants.

A few days later, Dad called me into his bedroom and locked the door. He had his own bedroom. Mom, my brother, and I slept in the second bedroom.

Dad started by playing games with me, and it was fun. Although the memories are somewhat fragmented, at some point he touched me and showed me how and where to touch him. Even though I didn't like doing it, I craved his approval, and he was my daddy, so I obeyed.

And I felt dirty.

I don't remember if that happened only once or several times. The next memory I have was after I turned seven. That's when he touched my breasts. "You're developing fast," he said. "You'd better be careful of boys. They'll take advantage of you."

By then we lived in the same apartment building, one floor above my father. I ran out of his apartment that time and into Mom's arms. "He—he touched me again."

"Stay here." She slammed the door and went downstairs.

I have no idea what she said, but after she came back I said, "I'm afraid he's going to get mad at me."

"He's not going to get mad at you," she said. "He shouldn't do things like that."

Thirty years later, I realized that Dad had destroyed my personal boundaries. Sad to say, it was only the first violation. Being that he was my father, it normalized being exploited and abused by men.

I believed all men were like him.

I'll tell you a little more about myself. I was born in North Miami, Florida. My brother, Daniel, is eighteen months older. Our mother is Finnish and our father was a Romanian Jew. I look like my mother, with blonde hair and a voluptuous figure. My first name, with the odd spelling, comes from my European heritage. My last name and hazel eyes show that I'm my father's daughter.

My parents divorced when I was three years old. Even after they were no longer married, my father wasn't out of our lives. As strange as it seems, my mother not only remained dependent on my father, but she continued to work for him all the years I was growing up. A typical arrangement was an apartment where Dad claimed the master bedroom and the three of us slept in the other.

Dad worked hard in real estate, where he bought and sold businesses. By the time I was born, he had become a millionaire. Despite that, he never enjoyed his wealth, and I don't think he was secure with the money he accumulated. He seemed constantly afraid that he would lose everything. Besides, Dad was cheap—very cheap—which I now realize was because of his fear of becoming poor again. Not only had he grown up during the Great Depression, it had also been an era of discrimination against Jews in America.

Because his life had been hard, I assume that's why he never gave me or my brother money for anything unless we begged. When he occasionally took the family out to eat—oddly enough, always at expensive places—he gave each of us a five-dollar limit, although a full meal would have cost at least twice that amount.

Before we went into a movie theater, we stopped at a convenience store and bought candy because it was cheaper. Even in those days, people weren't supposed to bring their own snacks, so we had to sneak our treats inside. I still have memories of those early years—strange, sad, and fragmentary—but they remind me of what an abusive childhood I survived, and I'm saddened to realize how Dad also abused my mother.

During my childhood, we moved often because we had no financial stability. Mom always seemed to be begging Dad for money. He often refused, even when it was for something like food or clothes.

Another factor about my father was that he had consistent interactions with those within the Mafia. But I have to say this for him: Dad wouldn't let them control him. The year before I was conceived, Dad argued with one of the Mafia bosses and refused to let them take over his business. A few days later, they bombed his office. Dad wasn't hurt, but only because he was late for work that morning. They didn't try again.

Dad's refusal to back down was one of the good things I learned from him. Long after I broke away from the sex trade, I figured out how to stand up for myself—it wasn't easy, but I learned. If I hadn't learned from his example, I wouldn't be alive today, fighting against this evil of human trafficking. I wasn't as courageous as Dad, who refused to be intimidated by the Mafia and kicked the boss out of his office. It took me a long time to take action, but ultimately I was able to stand up for myself.

And yet my life is also contradictory. The strong, determined part of my personality is there, but there has also been the victim mentality. I absorbed that by watching my mother's submission to Dad's cruel and demanding ways as well as giving in to his abuse and sexual advances.

For instance, my earliest memory of Dad is him putting me inside his car, locking the door, and walking away. I was too little to unlock the door. Because it's hot and muggy in South Florida in the summer, I began crying. I have no idea of the time factor, but my mother finally found me, opened the car, and took me into her arms.

Looking back, I wonder if Dad had some kind of personality disorder. However, my experiences set me up to be victimized. Learned helplessness and powerlessness entered my brain as a young child. I was taught to be dependent, and I looked for others' approval.

There was also a spiritual awareness in my life—not strong, but real. Around the young age of three, my mom told me about Jesus being God's Son and that God was my heavenly

Father. I didn't understand what she meant until one day when I was a little older. My dad was working outside on his car, and I heard a voice, which I learned to recognize as God's. That early memory stands out clearly, despite the years of cocaine in between.

I am your Father, the voice said.

Confused, I looked at Dad, who was perhaps twenty feet away. "Then who is that guy?"

He is your dad too, but I am your heavenly Father.

From that moment on, I knew I had a relationship with a different kind of Father, someone who was looking out for me. I didn't grasp what that meant, and it would be years before I threw off the victim mentality that I had learned from my earthly father who mistreated us.

It didn't take much for Dad to lose control, and little things set him off. Because his rules weren't consistent, I had no idea why or when he'd object or yell at me. My mother took the abuse, and I always knew who had the upper hand in our home and family. Ours was a male-dominated family, and we yielded to whatever the men wanted. No one said those words, but it was a learned form of behavior.

8

Enduring Rage

One memory stands out. Our family had gone to a restaurant. In those days, Dad took us out to eat quite often and in nice places. It seems strange because he was so tight with money, but I think he was showing off that he could afford to eat at fancy restaurants.

Mom sat across from Dad, and my brother, Daniel, sat across from me. Like many kids, my brother and I used to play games. As we had several times before, we wanted to see if we could sip our soda without our dad catching us. We did it because he had a rule that we weren't allowed to drink until we'd eaten because we'd lose our appetite. Whenever we sipped our soda and he caught us, he became angry. My brother and I became good at swallowing soda while Dad was looking elsewhere. Then Daniel and I would smile or laugh.

Dad caught me drinking my soda. "Stop that!" He became

so angry, he struck me with his fist and knocked me off the chair. "I told you not to do that! You never listen to me!" Once Dad started, he was like a violent animal and couldn't control his temper. "You kids are terrible!" He also swore at me.

As I lay crying on the floor next to the table, Dad's yelling grew louder. Other diners stared, and even the employees in the restaurant looked at us. It was obvious they were horrified, but no one knew what to do.

Knocking me to the floor wasn't enough for Dad. He stood over me and pummeled me. Because other patrons began making loud, harsh comments, he grabbed me and half-dragged me outside the restaurant. On the sidewalk, he continued to beat me—and most of the blows were on my face.

The more I cried, the angrier he became. "I'm sorry, Daddy! I'm sorry!" I kept yelling between sobs, but he was like a maniac. Nothing would make him stop.

Just then, a woman came up on the sidewalk and yelled, "The poor kid! Can't somebody stop this man?"

By then Mom and Daniel were also outside, and they were embarrassed and ashamed of his behavior. "Get in the car!" Mom yelled to me and pulled me away from Dad. "Just get in the car."

One of the waiters yelled, "Don't ever come back here!"

In the backseat of the car, my brother snickered because he had won the sneak-sipping competition. Then he must have realized I was hurt, and he stopped. I don't remember if he said anything, but he didn't tease me again that night. He became quiet, maybe because he realized that he could have been the one Dad slapped around.

All the way back to where we lived, Dad continued yelling and cursing at me. "It's your fault!" To my mind, he repeatedly used every swear word he knew. "How terrible for a daughter of mine to embarrass me and make me do things like that. Why do you do those things that you know will upset me? I am a businessman, not some kind of a bad person."

I cried from the pain of his blows, but even more because of his words. He made me feel that it had been my fault.

Mom tried to make it better and soothe him, but it seemed to have no effect. At one point, she turned around and said, "Don't make your father angry. Next time just obey him!" As young as I was, I felt she was trying to appease him more than excuse his behavior.

Despite the problems with Dad, I never questioned that my mother loved me. However, I don't think she understood my pain and turmoil then or for years afterward.

The most serious effect of Dad's frequent rages was that it made me fear men. The only way I knew to pacify him or other males was to let them have anything they wanted. In the years ahead, I related to men in the sex trade in the same way: I submitted. I hated myself for being in such situations, but I believed the lie that sex was all I was good for, that men always abuse, and that's how life was.

---- ☼ ----

Although my dad changed before he died, it didn't erase the painful memories of my childhood. For most of my life, I thought of him as the most evil man I ever knew.

And it wasn't only because of his treatment of me. He was like that with Daniel too. Even when my brother was a little kid, Dad would walk by and flick him in the head. I know it hurt him. I'm sure he made Daniel feel bad, because Dad used to say I was his princess and that I was special.

The evil went beyond our family. Many times I observed Dad deceiving clients. He bought and sold businesses and constantly used underhanded methods—always to his advantage. Lying was nothing to him. Mom was just the opposite. I think of her in those days as loving and naïve.

The older I got, the more estranged I felt from my dad, because I didn't want to be around his angry outbursts. For a few years on weekends, he'd take me to movies or teach me to play golf or tennis or how to shoot pool. I liked doing those things, but it wasn't worth it to take his verbal and sexual abuse.

Despite the abuse, by the time I was seven, I was working for Dad. I went to his office and did little things like sort papers, occasionally answer the telephone, or run errands, for which he paid me seven dollars a week. I absorbed the business language and learned how a small brokerage business functioned. That part of my early training would later pay off well.

After my parents' divorce, we moved often. We went from the house in Keystone Point to an apartment—really a duplex—in Miami's Biscayne Park.

More and more, I felt ashamed and didn't like anything about myself. I started gaining weight. Until then I had been thin and athletic. People said I was pretty, but that didn't help my self-esteem. The prettier I was, the more that meant I was unsafe; men and other people would want to take advantage of me.

Abuse happened again, and it's a terrible account. I'm not writing it for the shock effect, but because it taught me an invaluable lesson—I wouldn't be believed if I spoke up. Not only was it true in my life, but it's something I hear from other survivors of abuse and trafficking. Most of the time they don't speak up, but even when they do, no one believes them.

That time the perpetrator was my babysitter. I was seven years old, and she was a few years older than I was. One day after my mom left for work, she said, "Oh, we're going to play a game. Do you want to play one with me?"

"Okay," I said, trusting the older girl. Of course I didn't realize it then, but my childhood experiences created a vulnerability to trafficking recruitment.

The babysitter started touching me in various places and finally she performed oral sex on me. "Doesn't that feel good?" she asked.

I have no idea what I said, but I felt ashamed. She was a girl I trusted, and she did *that* to me. I felt dirty and, as strange as it may seem, I worried that if I told anyone, I'd get into trouble or they might think I was weird. *What am I supposed to do? This is somebody I trusted and now she's doing this strange thing to me. Am I going to get in trouble? Am I normal? What's wrong with me?*

When I told Mom, she had already had a few drinks and didn't give it the concern it needed. Or perhaps she didn't believe me and was dismissive because she didn't know how to handle it. Regardless, Mom didn't listen and did nothing about it.

The next time the girl came to our house and said she wanted to play, I said, "I can't play today," and closed the door.

As a result of being molested by a female, I would struggle with my sexuality for a long time, wondering if I was supposed to be bisexual or homosexual. Why did that happen to me?

A few days later when my mother asked about her, I said, "We got into a fight. I don't like her anymore and she doesn't like me."

A few months after the abuse incident, Mom invited that girl to my eighth birthday party and told me that I had to make up with her. I felt betrayed by Mom inviting my abuser—as if she had not heard a word I said.

"How could you do that?" I demanded.

"You have to make up with her. She's your neighbor and wants to be your friend."

"But Mom—"

"Whatever did happen," naïve Mom said, "she didn't mean anything bad."

I felt Mom had stopped defending me and instead defended the girl who molested me. Reflecting now as an adult, I realize that was also an especially bad period for Mom. My father was making life extremely difficult for her. But as a child, I was oblivious to her pain.

I hated not being able to stand up for myself. That's when I became aware of rebellion and anger entering into my life. Even now, I look back on that as the day my personality changed. I no longer lived in a good world—a safe world. I felt sick inside, and yet my mother wanted me to be friends with a horrible person who did something terrible to me.

Within days after my birthday party, I started missing school. As often as I could, I claimed to be sick. I didn't want to be around that girl, who attended the same school. I felt as if she now had permission to do whatever she wanted to me.

I missed school often—one time for three whole weeks. By then my mother had figured out that I faked being sick and was trying to avoid school altogether. She called the principal.

After Mom had gone to work, the principal drove to my house and knocked on the door. When I answered, he said, "Get in the car. You're going to school."

"I don't want to go."

He threatened to call the police, so I said okay and got into his little red sports car. He drove me to school. Even though not a lot of kids saw us pull into the parking lot, it was embarrassing. Word got around about what happened, and other girls teased me. They snickered because I wouldn't go to school like a big girl and had to be chaperoned by the principal. I was marked as an outcast, an outsider, like something was badly wrong with me.

I began putting on the pounds. At that age, I couldn't connect gaining weight and hating school with sexual molestation. Only later could I look back and realize how bad I felt about myself. Although I had been victimized by the neighbor girl and my father, like many children, I internalized everything as my fault. Something was wrong with *me*.

Perhaps I think of that incident with the principal because it exemplifies my craving for male acceptance that started early with the abuse I suffered from my dad. I used to follow my brother pretty much anywhere he went. Whatever he did, I tried to do it too. Certainly I was a nuisance, and he yelled at me or ran away from me.

Once I could no longer fake illness and didn't have any friends, I focused on my schoolwork. Through sixth grade I received a lot of praise for my scholastic ability, and I was almost a straight-A student. I was on the student patrol and got involved in school activities; however, during the summer after sixth grade, I changed. I lost all interest in school.

About that time, I began to hang out with the wrong group,

smoked Kool cigarettes, and had my first trafficking experience in the hotel. Still hanging around with the wrong kids, I moved from cigarettes to other drugs. I became "sort of" promiscuous in my pursuit of boys, wanting them to recognize me and my developing body. That is, I let boys touch me. I yearned for love and acceptance—by anyone—although I never allowed any boys to go beyond touching my body.

About that time, I started getting into serious trouble at school—rebelling, again faking sickness, and often just not caring.

——— ☼ ———

I've gone into detail about my childhood because it's important for parents to become aware of what's going on with their children as too many of them "check out" on their kids. That is, they're not emotionally available. They seem unaware of the problems or the changes going on in their kids' lives. They're not suspicious enough to investigate what their children say.

My mother was so emotionally beaten up by Dad and so dependent on him that we tried to appease him so he wouldn't lose control and lash out at us. I'm not blaming her. She was caught up in her own problems and heartaches, and she wasn't fully available for me.

I never doubted her love for me—and later she proved how much she truly loved me. Because she hadn't been able to protect me from Dad's volcanic eruptions, however, I felt as if it did no good to go to her with my problems.

Traffickers seek kids who are vulnerable because they feel unloved, alone, and misunderstood.

I was a perfect candidate.

9

From Bullying to Cocaine

After the kidnapping and attempted murder incident, we moved into another apartment. Mom did everything she knew to make me feel safe. We moved into the same building where Dad lived, and he was on the floor below us. It helped my still-dependent mother to feel better being near him.

But the move wasn't enough. Mom had saved my life and taken me away from Mary and the traffickers that networked throughout our hotel, but nothing changed inside me. I still had the same problems that made me vulnerable to predators. We lived in a new area, but I still felt lonely and insecure, and my self-esteem was at an all-time low.

Mom enrolled me at North Miami Junior High, which was the school for our area. Even though we no longer lived near Mary or any of those people, I feared they'd come looking for me. Had they wanted to do so, Mary and the others could have tracked me down. In fact, some experts have suggested that what happened next was not a coincidence.

I became timid and vulnerable, and by the time I entered seventh grade, I was an easy target for being bullied at school. I was scared every time I walked down the hall.

One day, an older Puerto Rican girl named Magdalene picked on me and yelled profanity at me just before my first class. A new friend said to me, "You have to stand up to her, otherwise this won't ever end and she won't back down."

The first day of Magdalene's bullying, I called my mother. After I told her what happened, she sent a taxi to pick me up. When I got home, I said to my mom, "I don't want to go back to school."

After I went into detail about the bullying, she said, "We'll switch schools."

Almost immediately after I turned fourteen, I started hanging out with kids that were the burnouts—kids like myself. We who had been abused, neglected, or felt unloved usually hung out with other kids with similar experiences. That's the one place we found acceptance and, in an odd way, a sense of identity.

Mom enrolled me in JFK Junior High School. Changing schools didn't solve my problems, because—for reasons I never knew—Magdalene changed schools too. In my new school environment, where I thought I could escape, once again I was tormented and bullied.

Even though I was terrified, I finally found the courage to stand up to the bully. The next day when I saw Magdalene and she began her usual harassment, I said, "That's enough! I'm not going to take that any longer from you!"

"Shut up or I'll beat you up."

"You got it! Three o'clock outside of school."

"All right," she said and brushed past me.

As I walked away, several kids who had heard us started cheering. "There's going to be a fight!" they yelled.

Just before the time to meet, I rushed into the bathroom. I stared into the mirror and said, "I can't do this." But I had to show up. It took a few minutes for me to calm down, but I finally went out in front of the school.

Magdalene wasn't there. I waited five minutes. By then, a large group of kids had gathered.

Five more minutes and she still hadn't shown up.

I didn't realize it, but I had grown taller and must have looked pretty powerful myself. I didn't have to fight her.

Magdalene never bothered me again.

In my new school, I began to hang around with Tanya and her clique. She was in the same classroom and sat next to me. We became friends, but it was more than that. I often went with her to her house. I didn't know the word then, but her family was highly dysfunctional.

Tanya had been sexually molested by her father, who was also a trafficker. She smoked pot and was moving into heavier drugs, which is a natural progression once the abuse takes place. When I was with her, she offered to share her marijuana with me. I didn't like pot, but once in a while I smoked a joint with her just to fit in.

Each morning before school, we got into the habit of standing in front of JFK and smoking until the school bell rang. On weekends, we went to a place called The Bridge, a hangout where many kids partied, located in Greynolds Park in North Miami Beach. At age fourteen, I shouldn't have been allowed to stay out at night, but I got away with it because I lied to my mother.

"Where are you going?" she asked each time.

"To Tanya's house." Or I might say to Dahlia's. I'd also tell her it would be late, but Dahlia's mom was there and it was safe (from what I understood safe to be). Sometimes I slept over, but I gave her the telephone number, which I knew she wouldn't use. The telephone number relieved any anxiety and Mom believed me. "All right," she said.

Tanya took me into her gang. It wasn't a good lifestyle, but it was better than staying alone at home. Many nights Tanya let me sleep on the sofa at her house. Her family gave us beer and let us hang out and do things big girls did, like stay up late, eat junk food, curse, and smoke cigarettes and pot.

I thought I had escaped a terrible home life with constant beatings and abuse from my father. But I escaped to something worse.

———☼———

Although I couldn't find words to explain it to myself, I knew something was weird with Tanya's family, and that was before I knew much about them. Her mom was drunk most of the time. Tanya told us girls who hung around with her (though not in so many words) that both her brother and her father had sexually molested her, and I was sure that it was still going on.

As our friendship grew and Tanya trusted me more, I learned another horrible truth: her dad was not only a sex trafficker, but he insisted she recruit her friends. Tanya did what she was told. Even though we didn't know what was going on, she chose a few other girls and me. We were ideal candidates: all of us were fourteen, all of us had come from abusive homes, and all of us were starving for affection.

I didn't understand what was going on at first, or perhaps I didn't want to know. Everything started out innocently, like going to her home for sleepovers and eating pancakes the next morning. After a few weekends, her dad invited a few of his male friends to the house while we were there.

Tanya's mother knew what they were doing and occasionally made some harsh comment. "Gonna hook these girls too, are you?" She was a drunk, so none of us paid any attention to what she said. Most of the time she was emotionally checked out.

The grooming process, although different, started just as before, slow and easy. And it was fun. The male friends were at least forty years old, and they seemed to like us. Being naïve, it didn't occur to me what was going on. And that's how the grooming process works—gradually learning to trust.

Why would we have suspected? Tanya lived in a nice apartment in an upscale neighborhood. Her mom cooked pancakes for us, and we played around the pool. We had no worries, plenty of food, and pot. It was a good, carefree life.

Then things changed. What began as simple sleepovers with other fourteen-year-olds turned out to be the deceptive structure of a family trafficking ring. They didn't start out by telling us they were planning to sell us on dates with her father's pedophile friends. Instead, they introduced us to the men who "dropped in for a visit."

The men spoke sweetly to us, gently (and inappropriately) caressing our shoulders or our hair. Even I could see the lustful look in their eyes that should be only for grown women. Because each of us girls had come from abusive homes where we never experienced what the safe love of a man looked like, we didn't see the exploitation looming. The affection seemed so sweet—which was a more potent drug than the cocaine they gave us to numb us to the reality of what was going on.

In the evenings, we sat around the sofa in the living room and just hung out. Those men started telling us funny stories and got us in a relaxed mood. They were in the fishing community, and they'd tell us things about what they did on their boats and made us laugh. They had a way of talking to us that made us want to listen—as if they wanted to be our friends and really cared about us.

Most kids don't care what adults talk about and feel adults aren't interested in listening to them. But those men seemed different—which was the purpose. They talked directly to us, entertained us, and were always friendly. To me, their direct interest meant they saw us as adults. We were wanted because they liked us.

One night Gary, a friend of Tanya's father, sat down next to me, close enough that our hips and thighs touched. Gary smiled at me before he said, "You have such beautiful hair." He leaned forward and stroked it.*

When I talk about this, I ask my audience, "Can you imagine that scene? Here was a girl who never had a kind, loving father. Then a forty-year-old man—someone old enough to be her father—wants to spend time with her, talks to her with

---

*Only later, after I received counseling, did I learn that hair is one of those areas that sexually arouse females. It's called an erogenous zone (they include the hair, the three sexual areas, and the mouth). I didn't know that, but I liked the way it felt—of course.

kindness and warmth, makes her laugh, and plays with her hair. Of course she's delighted and excited to have a father figure."

That's all it took and I was hooked. I didn't realize that love (or what passes for love) is the biggest, most addicting drug for needy kids like me.

During the time I was being recruited for sex, I was also being introduced to what would later be a big hook of deception in my life: the white stuff—cocaine. The first time I tried cocaine, it was only a sample on a tiny spoon. Although it's painful to write this, it started with a parent giving cocaine to her child's friend. I put it up my nose and it felt cold.

Almost immediately, I felt happy. Blissful. At peace. I forgot the pain of past abuse and loneliness. After that, the white stuff became my coping mechanism for dulling my senses to the true pain of my heart and the violations of my body and soul.

Every now and then, Dahlia, who was Tanya's best friend, and her mom offered me another sample. (Dahlia's mother was a dealer to our middle school.) The drug was always free, which is the best way to get innocents hooked. I never turned it down. After being introduced to coke, I used it almost every weekend, and we always had a party that included cocaine.

The only excuse I offer—and it helps me understand why people get addicted—is that it's a drug and it works. Temporarily. It doesn't solve anything. The problems and heartaches are still there after the drug wears off. As a kid, I didn't understand where the occasional use of cocaine would lead. I knew—and fully enjoyed—the temporary fix it gave me.

Adults know the addictive power, which is why Tanya's dad made sure we always had coke around. And not just us.

The male friends of Tanya's father did coke with us. It was like a party—we were all friends, and it seemed exciting to belong to such a sophisticated group with liquor and drugs.

Each time I went, I thought I was so lucky. They made me feel special—and often called me that. There was that word *special* again, but it was a term I yearned to hear.

"We're going to take care of you," Gary said casually one evening, "and you're going to do big-girl stuff."

"What do you mean, big-girl stuff?" I had no idea what he meant, or perhaps I needed to hear him say the words.

"I'm going to take you somewhere—a nice place—and you can live there and it will be your own apartment." Gary described how glamorous and sophisticated it would be. "And we can see you girls all the time. Right now your parents are in the way."

One time I asked, "Why can't you take us out on regular dates? You know, to dinner or to parties?"

"People wouldn't understand our kind of special love." He looked at me with such intensity, as if he loved me more than anything else in the world. And I believed him.

Each of us girls heard that kind of talk several times, and the men frequently painted a picture of the apartment they wanted us to have. "And it will be yours. Just yours," they promised.

We were fourteen years old and would have our own place. That sounded so mature and grown-up. As they explained it, we'd cook, clean the place, and take care of them. We wouldn't have to look for jobs, and best of all, it would be *our* place. We were girls who had never had anything of our own, not even our own bedroom, so we listened to their tantalizing lies.

We bought those lies—and they were lies. As I had to learn from experience, they didn't mean an apartment; they meant a brothel. By appealing to our desire to be special and to be *big girls*, they hooked us. We bought into everything they said. I felt I had been chosen—they picked *me*. Out of all the girls at JFK Middle School, they chose us.

We were special.

Just before we left that evening, they paid Tanya's father forty dollars for each of us. Then the men led us out of the apartment into a car.

I wonder why they're giving him money for us. Almost as soon as the questioning thought came, it was gone because everyone was cheerful and happy. We were going to have fun.

Maybe they're finally going to take us out to eat in a restaurant. All of us were excited, hardly able to wait for the adventure. Like me, the others also felt special and chosen.

Tanya got in the backseat with Lisa and me, and we squeezed together. As soon as we were inside the car, Gary said, "We need to blindfold you. It's part of the surprise."

I began to get scared, remembering Mary and her friends, and it no longer felt like fun. "Why do you have to put that blindfold on?" I said. "I don't like it."

"It's a secret location, and nobody can know where it is," the rough-looking man in front said as he tied the black cloths around our heads and made sure we could see nothing. (I would later learn that his position in the ring was what's called an enforcer. He enforced the rules and kept us in line.)

"Plus, we want you to be surprised. You'll love what you see," Gary said, making it sound like a game.

Because they didn't blindfold her, I whispered to Tanya, "Why are they doing this? Where are we going?"

She said nothing.

"Where are we going?" I asked Lisa.

"I don't know. I'm blindfolded too."

"Why can't you tell us?" I asked Gary. "Why can't we know before we leave?"

"You're in Broward County," the enforcer said. "That's all you need to know." He was someone I had never seen before. And he wasn't very nice talking to me that way.

I felt I had lost control of what was going on, as if I could no longer make my own choices. I was scared and nervous about where they were taking us. *Why doesn't Tanya have to wear a blindfold? What if I don't like the place where they are taking us? What if I can't find my way home? What if I never get back?*

I don't know how long we drove, but eventually the car stopped. Gary removed the black cloths from our faces. "This is it," he said excitedly and pointed to a building. "Your own place."

To my surprise, we were in a nice, middle-class, two-story building in a residential neighborhood. It didn't look scary; it was normal looking, although we did have the apartment at the very back of the complex. Because it wasn't a cheap, run-down place and there were other apartments, I told myself it was all right. If I tried to leave now, I reasoned, I didn't know where I was or how to get home.

"We're all going upstairs and you'll see your apartment." Then Gary added, "And something else: from now on, you don't have to go to school if you don't want."

I smiled. None of us liked school—and not having to sit in those classrooms every day added to the allure and anticipation.

Gary led us up to the second floor. All the time the men kept telling us about the good times we were going to have. "It will be worth the drive here. You'll see. You're special," Gary said. "We've met a lot of girls, but you and Lisa are different."

He opened the door to a three-bedroom apartment. The two men showed us around and said, "This is your place and this is where you're going to live."

The details are vague now, but we went into the kitchen and all three of us girls started to cook supper for our "family." Doing that made us feel mature and important. We felt we were responsible—big girls doing big-girl stuff.

Repeatedly the men said things like, "We're a family. We love each other, and you belong here with us. We've brought you so you can have all the freedom you want." We understood that freedom meant being away from the constraints of parents and school and any authority.

In the middle of the cooking and joking, something didn't feel right—a kind of unnamed anxiety made me feel uncomfortable.

"What's going on?" I asked Lisa.

"I'm not really sure. Let's go with this anyway. I know Gary isn't going to hurt us."

"It's okay," Tanya said. "Everything is cool."

Gary was nice and we liked him. More than that, we trusted him.

I don't remember anything happening that time. We fried chicken, made a big salad, and ate together. Everything seemed easy, and my discomfort began to dissolve.

Only later would I realize they had staged it exactly like that—the family together, loving each other and sharing a meal. It was the warm-up for what was about to happen next.

They kept asking questions and making us feel good. "Do you girls like this apartment? Won't this be a nice place to live? Nice neighborhood. And you don't have to pay any rent," Gary said.

By then I was hooked—as they knew I would be.

"Another thing you need to remember," the enforcer said, "is that only special girls get to live here. Girls like you."

Gary was our first "client." We bonded with him because he showered us with love and affection, while the other man was mean and harsh.

Gary was married and quite open about it. "And we have three great kids." He told us about his wife and said nice things about her.

"If you're married, why are you out here with us?" I asked. "Why would you do this if you're married?"

"My wife doesn't understand me, but I feel you do."

As pathetic as it sounds to me now, I believed him. I felt I understood him, which was the reason he liked me so much.

I have no idea how much school I missed, and I didn't care. Neither did Tanya or Lisa, my two friends. At first we missed only a day or two at a time, usually Friday and the following Monday. By then, all of us were using cocaine, so that took away our fear and we no longer wondered about our situation or what we were doing with our bodies or lives. Cocaine stopped all those concerns.

Gary made our relationship sound like something special and wonderful. Something I had never felt before. Young girls and older men—that was special.

Then came the serious awakening to what was going on.

10

Another Escape

isa and I were on the sofa. Gary had paid Tanya's dad again to have sex with both of us, but Lisa wanted to go first. She had deep feelings for him. So did I, because we thought he loved both of us. I'd never had a man in my life who showed me such kindness. He expressed love like a father and yet at the same time like a boyfriend, all wrapped into one.

That afternoon, I must have just come down after a heavy dose of the white powder. As I waited for Gary and Lisa, God spoke to me. Out of nowhere—I wasn't even praying. Yet when I heard those words inside my heart, I didn't doubt them.

This isn't love. You don't belong here.

I was confused.

The voice spoke again: *I have a plan for your life, and this isn't it.*

My heart began pounding and I didn't know what to do. *Get out of here. Now. Leave.*

I knew I had to obey. I had to get out of that apartment.

Until that moment—although I had occasional doubts, at least until the next cocaine fix—I believed the traffickers' lies and lived the lifestyle they wanted for me. I was doing coke regularly and denying to myself that it was wrong.

Just then, not only did I hear God speak, but I said to myself, "This isn't who I am. This isn't what I'm supposed to be doing with my life. My mom has no idea where I am. I don't know who I am anymore."

Usually a friend of Tanya's dad guarded the door whenever there was an appointment with a man. They said they wanted to protect us and make sure that nobody walking by became suspicious. That day, however, Lisa, Gary, and I were the only ones in the apartment. By then, they had gained our trust and we had become compliant and no longer asked about going out anywhere.

In a rare moment of clarity, *I knew.* I knew that everything the men had told us was a lie. They intentionally made us dependent on them so they could use us.

I stared at the door and no one was guarding it. I don't remember that ever happening before. I walked quietly to the door, unlocked the four locks, and softly closed the door behind me.

I hurried down the stairs and into the parking lot. I hoped someone would see me—a kind person to take pity on me. I had no idea how I got to that location or how to get home, because they still blindfolded us every time they brought us to the apartment.

I was totally disgusted with myself for being so stupid. I

was now in a horrible lifestyle and my life was in danger. I knew what would happen if I didn't comply.

God, I've been so wrong. Help me. This life—it's a big lie. I'm lost and I want to go home. I don't want to be a part of this. I don't want to live this way. And I don't want to be a drug addict. I don't want to do these things. This isn't love. Lord, I want to go home.

Tears began to flow as I stood in the parking lot, trying to figure out what to do. I was stranded in an unfamiliar neighborhood; the parking lot of the complex was immense. I didn't seem to be able to find my way out of there. I was lost and felt I had been kidnapped, and I was confused.

I didn't know how many days we had been in the apartment. But standing in the parking lot, the sunlight burned my eyes and the feelings of being afraid and lost overwhelmed me. I cried uncontrollably, and in that moment, I knew with utter clarity they didn't plan to take me home again.

I knew that if I didn't get away they would force me to go back and have sex with men. I didn't want to do that—not ever again. I wanted to be a good girl, and I wanted God in my life. Their deception—their false love—was turning me into somebody I never wanted to be.

I can't remember how many men there were or how many sex acts took place in that apartment, because parts of my memory have been traumatized and blotted out by the experiences. Yet in that parking lot, while I was in the deepest darkness, God reached down and rescued me.

Finally able to push away my tears, I walked around the parking lot, searching for some resident or passerby to help me.

Nobody came.

———☼———

Within ten minutes after I left the apartment, Lisa had gotten dressed and was outside looking for me. "Kat, it's your turn. You'd better get back in there."

"I don't want to. This is a lie. They're lying to us."

"Gary loves us—"

I continued walking toward the rear of the parking lot.

"Come on back," Lisa said.

I shook my head. "I won't go back."

"Hey, come back," Lisa pleaded. "It's not that bad. We can do this—"

"They've been lying to us—Gary doesn't love us—none of them do. Don't you see that? What they gave us isn't love." In my heart the lie had been exposed, and I wasn't going back. "Come on, Lisa, wake up. Don't you realize that they've been lying to us the whole time? They *don't* love us."

"No, no, that's not true. Gary loves me. He told me so."

Gary came outside then and I argued with both of them. "I don't want this kind of life!" I screamed.

"Aw, come on inside," Gary said. "Calm down and then we'll talk about it." He meant he'd give me cocaine to destroy my resistance.

"I'm not going to do this anymore," I said, surprised at my own defiance. "I'm not going to live like this. This is not the way life should be. You stay if you want, Lisa, but I'm done. I'm done with this and I'm going home."

"No, you can't. They're not going to let you go. Don't you get it?" she said. "You can't walk away. Besides, if you leave, you're going to mess things up for everybody. All of us will get in trouble."

"I don't care. Let them do whatever they're going to do."

"What if your mom finds out what you've been doing?"

Before I could answer, Gary said, "Don't go, Kat. I love you." His voice was as sweet as always. "I really, truly love you."

"I don't want to hear it, and I'm not going to listen. I want out of here. Now."

I kept on talking that way, and finally Gary must have gotten sick of me. "Okay," he said. "Go then."

Lisa still didn't want to leave. She truly felt Gary loved her, so she stayed.*

Back then, none of us knew about trafficking. If it had happened today, Tanya's father would have ended up in federal prison for twenty years for selling his daughter and her friends.

Gary drove both of us back to Tanya's home, and no one said a word on the long drive. This time there were no blindfolds. Just as we got out of the car, Gary said, "I'm going to let you go because I love you." I almost believed him until he added, "But I don't want any trouble."

Gary grabbed my arm and we went inside. Once there, Gary didn't yell at me and was again a kind man. But Tanya's dad and the enforcer were irate. They yelled at me and threatened me.

"Sit down!" Tanya's father said. "We're going to let you go home. But not before you sit in that chair and we tell

*Months later Lisa became pregnant by Gary. Because Lisa was only fourteen, her mother had Gary arrested for child abuse.

you exactly what's going to happen to you if you ever tell anybody."

They scared me, and I couldn't stop shaking. They threatened me and my parents if I ever said anything to anyone about them. "And we'll kill you if we have to do that," the third man said.

Because of my previous experience with Mary's friends, I had no doubt that they would if I ever told.

"We know where you live. We know your brother, your teachers, and your friends. We also know how to take care of your parents."

It was a horrible, frightening situation, and even after all these years, it's painful to think about the things I did and had to experience. Even worse was the shame.

None of us girls realized it, but we had become prostitutes. They hadn't given us money, although they had paid Tanya's dad for us, but they provided enough coke to keep us numb to the reality of the life.

They intimidated me so much, I didn't speak about that experience for twenty years.

After they scared me, Tanya's father allowed me to make a monitored phone call to my mother. She and my dad came to get me.

"Why did you skip school?" she asked. "Where have you been? I was worried about you!"

Mom was yelling at me and Dad was yelling at her. I didn't say much, and I certainly didn't tell them about the apartment, the sex, and the drugs. If they found out, I was sure those men would kill them and me as well. I had to protect them. My mom had enough problems dealing with my father; I was not going to give him more reason to hurt her.

"You're degraded and you lose your dignity," I tell kids today, "and you don't know who you are or what you are. But you know you're not living right. You know what your mother or father taught you. And those values that you were brought up with as a kid fly out the window.

"That's when you realize you've become somebody's property. You're so addicted to drugs and the lifestyle, intimidated and living in so much fear, you'll do whatever they tell you."

I wish someone had talked to me that way.

— ☼ —

I had heard God say he had a plan for me and he wouldn't let me go. I couldn't understand how I had been trapped a second time into a sex trafficking ring, but I had. And the shame increased.

God, in his faithfulness, saved me for a second time. But something else happened on that car ride home from Tanya's house with my mom and dad fighting in the front seat. I knew I had changed; I was different. That lifestyle had become normal.

At age fourteen, I had lost my virginity to rape. I tried to have a normal relationship with a boy I thought I loved, but I only interacted with him as being his property. There are so many aftereffects of being trafficked; we have to relearn how to relate to men and to life. And it takes a lifetime to recover.

As much as I wanted to know and serve God, I had so many hurt and unhealed parts that I didn't know how to trust God to set me free. I was no longer a sex slave, but I wasn't free. And because I wasn't healed emotionally, I was still susceptible to traffickers. It was as if I had become an adult overnight.

I felt angry—angry at myself, angry because I couldn't tell my mother, and angry that she had believed my lies and let me go with Tanya. In my heart, I blamed her for most of what happened. Why didn't she ask more questions? Didn't she care about what those people were doing with us girls?

I was angry at the school authorities. Why had they allowed such terrible things to happen? School was supposed to be a safe place, but it wasn't safe for me anymore. After experiencing bullying, drugs, and then trafficking, I knew darkness could dwell anywhere. If such terrible people could lure innocent kids into sexual activity and dope, how could I be safe?

My life felt horrible. I didn't want to go back to that brothel apartment, but I wasn't happy at home. I didn't tell a soul what happened. I was ashamed. "Everything's okay," I told myself and anyone who asked where I had been.

But everything wasn't okay.

In fact, nothing was okay.

I began to feel suicidal. Was life worth living? Who would care if I died? I didn't think about God's voice telling me about a plan. I didn't want a plan; I didn't even know if I wanted to live. I was still scared, but I went to school and tried to be like everyone else—even if I didn't feel like anyone else.

My first day back at school after leaving the brothel apartment, I saw Dahlia and Tanya. They had returned to school too. Several times throughout the day they tried to entice me to go back with them, but I wasn't interested. I was deathly afraid that they would try to do something to me like Mary's friends had done.

"You're a narc," Dahlia said as she walked up to me my

first day back at school. "I know you. You're going to tell. You can't hang around us ever again. You can't be a part of our group. And you remember what Tanya's dad said would happen to you if you told, right?"

"I'm not going to tell anyone, I promise. Please, I just want you to leave me alone."

"You will talk because you've turned against your friends."

"No, I promise. I won't—"

"Okay, you can prove it. Hold my cigarettes for me." Without giving me a chance to answer, she thrust them into my hand and hurried on as the bell rang.

Something deep down inside of me felt terrible about accepting those cigarettes. Dahlia didn't smoke, so that seemed strange. But then, I thought, maybe she's smoking now and doesn't want anyone to know.

About an hour later, the school superintendent called me into his office. "Do you have something in your purse that shouldn't be there?"

"No, of course not."

He held out his hand for my purse. "May we look inside?"

"Sure."

He sorted through things, and after he pulled out the cigarette package, I said, "Those aren't mine."

He opened the package anyway. Only then did I realize he had been told what the package contained. He pulled out a joint that had been hidden in the back. "Whose is this?"

"That's not mine." It wasn't mine, and I wasn't going to get in trouble. At the moment, it still hadn't occurred to me that Dahlia had set me up.

"Really? Well, if they aren't yours, we have to conduct an investigation. I'm sorry, Katariina, but until we find out or you can prove otherwise, you're suspended." His voice made it clear that he didn't believe me.

As I left his office, Dahlia and Tanya were sitting in the outer office. As I passed, we didn't speak to each other, but their hardened faces told me everything. Their angered looks seemed to shout, "This is only the beginning of what's going to happen if you tell anybody."

I knew what message they were sending me. I didn't talk to either of them again, but they spread rumors all through the school about what a bad person I was. They said I took drugs and gave them to others. They told about some of the sexual things I had done—except, naturally, they weren't involved. They said I had told on them and that I was a narc. I was ostracized.

To her credit, Mom understood and did the most natural thing: she transferred me to another school. There were kids there who knew kids at JFK, so it didn't matter that the new school was in North Miami Beach. Kids talk. Even though there were addicts in that school, no one seemed to focus on them. It wasn't long until kids called me a narc and whispered about me.

I felt miserable and hated going to school. Every day was torture, and no one liked me. That may not have been true, but that's how I felt. In my pain and misery, I told Mom, "I'm not going back. I don't care what you do, I'm not going back."

I dropped out about two months into the ninth grade. Mom tried homeschooling me, but neither of us had the self-discipline to follow through.

Unable to cope with me, Mom became depressed. "I don't

know how to deal with this," she said more than once. I had changed, and she saw the deterioration in me. As a last resort, she enrolled me in what is called a preparatory school in Miami, but it was actually a school for troubled kids.

In some ways, that school was worse than JFK. Everywhere I went in the facilities, kids were on drugs—far more than I had seen in my previous schools.

I hated the kids at that school as well, and didn't feel there was a safe place for me. Suicidal thoughts kept racing through my mind. I met other kids who were on drugs and thought, *Oh, that's all I am—one of them.*

After a few weeks, I couldn't take sitting in a classroom. I became rebellious and argued with my teachers. I yelled at my mother—something I hadn't done before. I didn't understand myself, and yet I couldn't be the girl I had been. Something inside of me had changed. "I can't sit in a regular classroom and listen to all those stupid rules from adults," I told my mother. I still seemed to be the target of bullies everywhere I went. My self-esteem fell even lower.

Mom tried so hard to help me, but I sank down deeper and deeper into the life of a troubled teen.

Mom gave up on the prep school. In fact, I think she just gave up altogether. It was only a matter of time before another trafficker picked me up.

11

Enslaved . . . Again

was still the same needy, insecure, frightened girl I had
been before I met Tanya's father and got hooked on drugs.
Only now I had even worse sexual abuse and exploitation added into the mix. Despite God's help, nothing had
changed inside me.

So it happened again—right in our apartment building.
By then I was fifteen and had dropped out of any kind of
schooling. About that time, Jan, a friend from my school
days, came to see me. She was only a few months older than
I was.

After I promised not to tell anyone, she told me her dad had
been molesting her. I was so concerned about my friend going
back into that situation, I broke my promise and told Mom
what happened to Jan. In turn, she insisted on my calling the
abuse hotline. The authorities placed Jan in a group home.
After two weeks, she ran away and visited our apartment again.

"It was terrible," she said. "I won't go back. I don't know where I'll go, but I won't go back to that group home."

Mom and I took pity on Jan and invited her to live with us. She became my best friend. Like me, she had dropped out of school. With abuse and exposure to drugs in both our backgrounds, it was just a matter of time before the two of us were recruited.

Jan was with me one day when we met a man on the elevator in our apartment building.

"My name is Marco," he said and started talking to us. He was a short, older Cuban man, and either he told us or we figured out that he was seventy years old. We lived on the fourth floor and so did he. He was friendly, and we chatted a little. Just as we got off the elevator, he asked, "Do you live with your mom and dad here?"

"No, just my mom," I answered, thinking it was a seemingly innocent enough question.

"In my apartment, I have *café con leche*—coffee with milk." He smiled and asked, "Would you like that?" His voice was smooth and sounded like a gentle, elderly man.

In retrospect, I think he needed only to look at Jan and me to sense our vulnerability. It never occurred to us that despite being seventy years old, Marco was a pimp living on the same floor of our apartment building. As a pimp and trafficker, he was constantly looking for fresh meat.

"You have a father, is that correct?"

"Yes, but he's always busy working." I pointed to Jan and said, "She lives with us."

"Ah, I see. And does your father not mind that you are not in school?"

"He doesn't care."

At the time, I didn't realize that I had given him all the information he needed. Jan and I were perfect candidates.

"You need someone to whom you can talk at times, yes?" Before I could answer, he said, "You must come by my apartment. I will be there to listen and to talk with you. Anytime."

I smiled and wondered what kind of man he was. It was weird and creepy that the old guy actually thought we would go to his house just to talk to him and drink *café con leche*.

But then he said something else just before he left us. "You seem like nice girls but very, very lonely. Do you have anybody to listen to you?"

"Not really," Jan said. I only shook my head.

"You don't need to be afraid of me. I'm retired, and I'm in my apartment all day. I live in this building and I get lonely to be with other people." As we continued talking, he made us feel that he was a harmless old man.

"Do you like the white stuff?" he asked softly and innocently before he smiled at us.

Jan and I understood. He was offering us cocaine, which to us meant he was cool. Even as we parted and I acted like I wouldn't see him again, I knew differently. I'm sure he did as well.

Neither of us worked, so we had no money. Because both of us had a prior exposure to that drug, we hadn't expected an addiction to come as a result. Neither of us was so addicted that we had to have it every day. We were mostly weekend users. By going to parties, we made our connections. We would stay out until early the next morning after we had come down from our highs.

But the lure of the white powder drew us. That same day we went to Marco's apartment, which was on the same floor but on the other side of the building. He was nice to us, very caring and kind.

And he gave us cocaine. Free.

At first we went over once or twice a week. And each time Marco gave us free drugs. Both of us knew how difficult it was to get because neither of us had money. In those days, the cost was sixty to eighty dollars for a gram of coke, depending on how good it was.

"I like doing this for you," he said when we asked about money. "You don't need to pay me anything."

He was nice and inoffensive. Because of my previous experience, I was leery of him in the beginning. Yet he never showed any indication of being unsafe. Three months passed before he won my trust.

We spent our days sitting in his apartment doing cocaine when we should have been in school. Although Jan and I never discussed it, deep inside I hated myself for falling into the daily use of drugs. We were losers—and I also knew we were hopeless and lost.

One thing, however, troubled me. "It seems odd that you would give us free drugs. It's expensive. Why do you do that?" I asked Marco several times, wondering what he wanted in return.

"Whenever you get money, you can pay for the drugs if you like," he said with indifference in his voice. "I get lonely with no one to talk to. I like both of you because you're nice girls, and I feel less lonely when you're here to talk to me."

We liked hearing that we mattered to somebody, and Marco never did anything to make us suspicious. He wasn't a user, but he provided for us. The only odd note, as I look back, was that occasionally young men visited his apartment while we were there. They were in their twenties and thirties and delivered coke to him. Each time he introduced them and said they were his sons or implied they were related. Every visitor was introduced with the broad explanation of *family* or *cousin.*

Before long we figured out that Marco was a dealer, but we didn't realize he dealt in more than drugs. When the young men came to buy or make some kind of deal or transaction with Marco, they did it quietly and quickly—in and out. After that, other visitors came to the apartment. They put their money on the table, and Marco handed them small bags of the white powder. Simple. Not much talking because both parties knew what they wanted.

A few minor-aged girls showed up—either living there part-time or just hanging out for the day and getting high. Who they were wasn't clear to me, and with drugs in my system, I didn't care. At the time, I didn't think about that—I didn't want to. I was getting all the cocaine I needed. Marco didn't do anything to us or ask anything of us. Getting our drugs was all we cared about.

One of the young men began showing an interest in Jan. Each time he came, he stopped and chatted with her. They developed a sexual relationship. I didn't care because I was getting fatherly love and cocaine from Marco.

———☼———

I continued spending my days in Marco's apartment, doing bumps of coke. By that time I had become totally compliant. I didn't care about anything except getting another hit.

Daily Marco said he loved me. "We are family, you and I," he said. "When you are sad, I am unhappy."

The girls in this lifestyle—and boys as well—are victimized repeatedly. Traffickers focus on what we need in order to enslave us. In my case, that meant my unmet father need and a yearning to be loved. We believed what we were told because we *wanted* their words to be true. Because we thought so little of ourselves, we became easy victims and readily accepted their lies.

A few of those who are victimized in trafficking are business smart. After they're lured into the trade, they determine, "I'm going to get paid for this," and they do. They're still victims, but the traffickers use a different tactic with them. They lure them with power and money. "Yes, that's fine," they say. "You're going to be my best girl. You're number one. You'll run those other girls."

Especially for those who have never had control over anything in their lives, who have known only domination by men, it can be a heady experience. They usually don't see themselves as victims like the rest of us. Money and power blind them to reality.

The smartest of the "best girls" become like wives. That is, they're no longer for sale. They recruit others—as Mary did—and they seek out other vulnerable kids. If Mary told me the truth, she was nineteen years old and was already recruiting thirteen-year-olds.

———— ☼ ————

Some people might ask why I was so stupid to get caught in trafficking more than once. But those who ask don't realize the pain and lack of self-worth in those of us who are victimized. The traffickers make promises; they profess love and protection—the things we don't get from our homes. They give us just enough cocaine and elusive promises so that we remain compliant and they can dominate our lives. As I would learn much later, until something changes inside us, we're vulnerable and able to be manipulated by people who want to use our bodies for their gain.

Only a miracle could take me out of that lifestyle.

12

Unsuspected Predators

Marco set it up for us to go out on dates with clients. Until then, men always came to us. Because I didn't understand, Marco explained a date.

Marco had Reggie take Jan and me out for a drive. Reggie was about twenty-five, good looking, and he was nice to us. He owned a white Mustang, all souped up with loud bass on his stereo and fancy rims on his wheels. We drove around until he pulled up alongside the Fontainebleau Hotel in Miami Beach. "You're going to start going to nice places like that."

He showed us other places—always only the best, most expensive places, although he didn't take us inside.

He talked constantly about how wonderful our life was going to be. "We're going to show both of you how to make money, have dates, and enjoy yourselves." And I loved hearing those things. Did I believe them? I wanted to believe.

As he drove us around, Reggie wanted to check us out, and he asked me questions. By now I understood why, although I was so high I answered anyway.

"Is there anyone in your life who looks out for you?"

"My mother just isn't there for me," I said. "I have a brother, but he's into his own world. My parents are divorced, and my dad is mean."

"Do you go to school?"

"Not any longer," I said. "I had some problems with school. You know how it is, so I dropped out."

After a few more questions, the driving around ended. Just before we went back to Marco's apartment, he said, "So here's how the dates work. You go on dates that we set up for you. All you have to do is go with them and do whatever they want. Easy."

"What if I don't want to go with a guy?"

"Oh, well, you'll want to because they are nice men. All are good-looking guys with lots of money who will treat you well."

"Who are they?"

"People Marco and I know," he said in such a way that it seemed insignificant. "We'll watch out for you because you're special. We don't want anything bad to happen to you. We love you, and we'd never send you with anybody who's not good."

Reggie was saying all those nice-sounding words, and I was strung out on drugs. Half of what he said didn't get through anyway. The longer I was in trafficking, the more desensitized I became. That lifestyle started to feel normal, and I even began to believe it was harmless. Not once did I ever call it what it was; I never considered myself to be involved in prostitution. I was going on a "date" with friends and good men who showed me attention. At fifteen, love was what I was looking for and all I wanted.

Reality slowly sunk in, because not all of the men were pleasant. Some abused us—insulting us and yelling at us. Sometimes they became violent and hit us. Many were emotionally sick themselves. I learned early that if I cried, that enraged my dates and they'd get angry or beat me up even more. Sometimes they ripped off my clothes.

To these men I wasn't a person, I was a commodity. I was a piece of meat, not even a child. I had lost my childhood innocence, dignity, and self-respect before I started going on "dates."

In time, I began to see myself the way the customers saw me—as nothing. And that's what I felt I was: nothing.

13

Fearing Paco

By the time I met Paco, I was already under Marco's control. I didn't want to admit that reality to myself. I would tell myself, "I can walk away from this whenever I want." Or sometimes I'd say, "Until I kick the coke habit once and for all, I'll go along with this."

A few dates with any man, and then it was over. Lasting love never came for me.

The man I most remember—and who still makes me shudder—was Paco. He was in his thirties. He came to the apartment several times and smiled at me. He flirted a bit, but I ignored him. He had lesions and scars on his face, which made him appear ugly. He was Latin or Caribbean and had a tan. Most of the time he wore a harsh look that would make any child want to run the other way when he approached.

One day Marco mentioned him. "You know Paco likes you, don't you?"

I shrugged because I didn't care.

"He wants you. He talks about how much he likes you, how pretty you are. He wants to be your date."

"Whatever." I wasn't attracted to him, but we didn't get to pick; we simply did whatever Marco told us.

The following night, Paco picked me up at the apartment, I got into his van, and we drove away. He seemed nice enough, although he didn't say much; he spoke broken English. After a time he said, "I drive into this parking lot."

He stopped, climbed into the back, and told me to come back there with him. As soon as I was in the back of the van, he became violent. He shoved me and started pulling off my clothes. The other girls had told me stories of rough treatment—which was really rape—but I was surprised because most of the men I went out with were nice and caring.

I started to cry.

"Shut up!" he yelled in Spanish, calling me *puta* (whore). "You're a cheap whore. I have you all to myself, I can do whatever I want to you."

I cried silently and thought, *Yes, that's all I am.* But I still resisted and couldn't stop crying. It was more than the pain of what he was doing; it was also the pain of knowing I was a *puta*.

"What's going on in there?" Some man in the parking lot must have heard my cries because he banged on the doors. "I hear screaming. Is she okay?"

Paco covered my mouth and yelled back, "Mind your own business!"

The man banged on the door several more times, and when

Paco didn't respond, he stopped. As soon as Paco was sure the man had gone, he knocked me backward and crawled up to the front of the van. He started the engine and pulled away.

He yelled at me and cursed me, but I didn't care. After I tried to dress in my torn clothes, I got into the passenger seat—as far from him as possible.

In his angry mood, Paco drove crazily through the streets. As soon as we reached the apartment, he came to an abrupt halt. "Get out, *puta!*" he yelled, and called me more names.

I didn't hesitate. I rushed inside and to my apartment. I was upset, but I made up my mind that I wouldn't let it bother me. I took a long shower and tried scrubbing away the memories of that night.

I'm never going on one of those dates again. Not ever.

But within hours, the urge—the gnawing need for cocaine—returned. Drugs like cocaine will take people places they never planned on going. By noon I was in Marco's apartment for another fix.

I thought that was the end of Paco. I was wrong.

Marco saw that he was losing me, and that made it time to trade me—although I didn't understand what was happening. Marco introduced me to his "associate," Julio, whom he said wanted to present a wonderful opportunity to me.

Marco had earned our trust because he always seemed to care about us. I never thought that he was a pimp or could be selling children. Those of us in that world didn't think much about such things anyway.

Marco had told us that Julio owned a lot of property in an upper-class neighborhood. Even though I was only fifteen and didn't have a license, I had borrowed my brother's car. Jan and I stopped at the address Marco gave us, which was in front of a huge apartment high-rise. Despite what I knew deep within, I was impressed with the building and the neighborhood.

The place was spectacular, which was the reason Marco sent us there. Inside, Marco was waiting for us, and he introduced us to Julio.

Like Marco, Julio was Cuban, but there the similarity ended. He was a large man, perhaps fifty years old, well-groomed and well-dressed. He looked like a prosperous businessman.

Once at the apartment, Julio wanted to talk to each of us alone in his bedroom, first Jan and then me. Jan and I looked at each other as she went in. We knew each other well enough that we didn't always need to use words. She gave me the slightest nod, and the determination on her face made it clear that we were together and we wouldn't let Julio manipulate us.

When he got Jan alone, he told her how special she was and that he wanted her to be his top or best girl. He did the same thing with me.

The offer to be top girl (nowadays called the "bottom") was his way of introducing Jan and me to the process of moving to another trafficker/drug dealer. Even though these people treated us politely (then at least) and frequently told us how they loved us, in the depths of our hearts we began to realize they were lying. But we were caught once again in that invisible chain of slavery. They continued to use drugs to keep us in line.

On some level, I understood the setup. Men at the top, like Julio, use people like Marco to lure children into the web and make us feel accepted. After that, the lower-level younger men make us fall in love with them. That way they can use us to do the work and keep feeding us drugs so we don't ask questions. And we keep coming back for more drugs.

Trafficking usually works like a pyramid scheme. The top people are highly respected, some are even in politics. For example, Julio was a businessman, more like the type of top-level drug dealers we see portrayed on television. And the traffickers go from the top down to the lower-level drug dealers and street-level pimps. I've also learned that child protection workers, those within the school system, and even retired detectives have been involved in selling children into the sex trade.

Everybody profits except the girls and boys and their families whose lives are ruined.

After Julio took Jan into the room and closed the door, I asked, "What is he doing with Jan? Is she okay?"

"He's just talking to her," Marco said in his soft, fatherly voice. "He's explaining about the opportunity she has. You'll get a chance for the same opportunity, but I don't know if you're up for it. She'll probably take it because she's smarter."

I felt I had to make Marco know that I was as sharp as Jan. I wasn't going to lose a good opportunity to live in a high-rise like this. I didn't have anything, and they offered me a wonderful, exciting lifestyle; I didn't want to miss out on it.

As I would learn, that was another of the major strategies they use, especially in the beginning. They make the girls feel as if they have to compete with each other.

After perhaps thirty minutes, Jan came out, and Julio

immediately asked me to go into the room with him. Another of their strategies was to not let us talk to each other and compare what Julio said.

I called out to Jan, but Julio stepped in front of her. "No, no, come on in now! I'm ready for you. Right now."

Jan barely shook her head and the look warned, "Be careful."

He pointed to the bed and I knew he wanted me to lie down. "Face down." I had enough coke in me not to resist, so I obeyed. He began to massage me, but I didn't like what he was doing.

"Take off your shirt!"

I complied and felt even more uncomfortable.

I would have gotten up and walked out, but I reminded myself that Julio had given us cocaine. As strange as it may seem, I felt I owed him for the free coke.

I don't know if I should do this, I was thinking. *He's so old. This is gross.*

After a few minutes, he said gruffly, "You want to have sex?"

"No."

"Oh, okay." He paused momentarily because I think he realized that I had wised up to what he was doing with Jan and me. I wasn't giving in easily.

He sat beside me on the bed and said, "As you probably know, I have this business." He started to lay out his business plan and tried to proposition me. In broken English, he said, "I give you some of my business. See, if you get other girls involved, you can make money—lots of money. I give you half."

I understood. Julio was offering me the chance to become the top girl—by recruiting other girls.

Julio tried to make it sound glamorous and exciting. "See,

you have only to make dates. You get friends involved—and a good-looking girl like you must have many friends. That's all you do. You have sex with me once in a while—you know, whenever I want, but nothing else."

That last sentence was a deal breaker for me. "No."

"I give you money—a lot of money. As much coke as you want. You can have a nice, big car. A house—yes, I give you a house—and a lot of new clothes."

He knew exactly how to manipulate me. Like any teenager, I never seemed to have enough clothes. He knew exactly what to say to lure girls like me and get us hooked for life. And yet I couldn't bear the thought of recruiting other kids and ruining their lives.

As Julio was trying hard to sell me on that lifestyle, his voice grew louder. "But if you don't do this, the supply of coke stops. Right now you don't pay for it. You refuse, and no more freebies."

I understood the manipulation. He was saying that either I did what he asked or no more cocaine, and his threats weren't empty.

I had already become addicted, and he knew that.

"Let me think about it," I said. I got off the bed, put my shirt back on, and he let me leave the room.

Julio was right behind me. He tried to put on the charm with a big smile, but it didn't work. Back in the main room again, he asked, "Which of you is the smart one?"

Marco, in his softer voice, said, "It is a good opportunity. For *one* of you."

"I have to go," I said. "I borrowed my brother's car, and if I don't get it back soon he's going to beat me up. He doesn't know I have it."

"But you can't go yet," Julio said.

In that moment, I realized something. One girl alone is powerless and easily manipulated. Because Jan and I were together, we were stronger. If we joined forces then we could defeat them. While they weren't looking, she grabbed more than a gram of coke—and put it in her pocket.

As we walked out to the car, I said, "We don't have to do anything here."

"That stupid Julio," Jan said. "He thinks he's going to get one over on us."

Because Julio repulsed me with his offer, several days passed before I went back to see him. I didn't want anyone to be in control of my life, and I certainly didn't want to have sex with old men. But then again, I was only fifteen years old with no schooling, no job, no car, no license, and no life of my own.

Julio continued to try and sell us on "the life," or as I call it, "the lie." He invited us to go out on his boat. During the day we did all the coke we wanted while drinking and cruising on Miami's intercoastal waterway and passing by the big cruise ships.

After a few days, we had used up all the coke Jan stole, so I borrowed my brother's car again and we went to one of the homes that belonged to Julio. To my surprise, I saw Beth, a girl from my elementary school. Now, seven years later, she was strung out on drugs. No longer beautiful, she looked spent. Worn out.

I looked around and saw almost no food in the kitchen and asked about it.

"Why do we need food when we have coke?" Beth said and laughed.

She finally stopped talking and walked away. Julio came up to me and said softly, "Don't listen to her. She's nothing but a coke whore."

That's how you refer to her, I thought, *and that's what you think of us.*

"She snorts too much coke," he said. "Don't become like her."

I smiled, but inside I thought, *You made her like that.*

—————☼—————

A few minutes later, probably after a fresh fix, Beth came back to where we were. "Come and live here with me. You get nice clothes, you get your own car, and you get money. You don't have to go to school ever again. We can be sisters."

I shook my head; at least I think I did. The rest of the afternoon and evening were a blur until there was a knock on the door.

My next memory is that Julio opened the door. Paco came inside.

"What's he doing here?" I whispered to Beth. "I can't stand him."

Before she could answer, Julio came over to me. "He's here for you, Kat."

"I don't want to go with him."

The drug dealer looked at me and said flatly, "I don't care what you want. You're here for him. So get upstairs and do what you're told to do." He used a lot of profanity as he pushed me toward the stairs.

At that moment, I realized that my life no longer belonged

to me. The façade that they made up was only an outward show with no reality behind it. A deep disappointment and sense of betrayal set into my heart as I struggled to get up the stairs. I didn't argue or try to fight after that—it would have done no good. I knew who I was and how worthless I had become. Besides, I knew from my upbringing that women were powerless. Men always had the upper hand, so I gave in.

Paco grabbed my arm and pushed me into the room. He was violent, and I wasn't going to do anything to help him. He started tearing off my clothes, exactly as he had done before.

Just then I caught a glimpse of my face in the mirror. I saw a lost, confused child. *I'm a little girl. I'm not even grown yet and this is all I am. These men will use me however they want. I have no control, I have no money, and I don't even know where I am or how to get home. How did I get in this position again?*

As I stared at the lesions on Paco's face, I thought, *This is all I'm ever going to be. I've got to do what they tell me to do.* I cried while that man violently pushed me onto the bed, and inside I continued to plead for God to help me. Paco became angrier, and I didn't know what he was capable of doing. People like him who used children and young women to satisfy their sick sexual appetites created and sustained an industry of disposable people.

Like many of the others, Paco carried a gun, and I worried that he might use it on me. He saw me crying but he didn't care; he just kept having his way with me.

As strange as it seems, just then I heard the voice of God say once again, *I have a plan for you, and this is not it.*

You can't want me, God. Look at me. I'm nothing. I gave up on myself, so why should you care? I thought about my miserable life and where I was. *No one knows where I am, and I'm sure no one cares. Everybody has given up on me. My friends, my dad, my family, my counselors at school, and society have given up on me. My mom is constantly mad at me because I give her so much trouble. I'll live here and I'll do whatever they tell me, because I don't have anything and I'm nobody. God, give up on me, because I give up on myself.*

Right then, I heard the voice of God speak to me for the third time: *I have a plan for you, and this isn't it. You are not going to be what they want to make you!*

God, I gave up on me. You should too! Leave me alone. Stop talking to me.

Just then, in the middle of the sex act, Paco became sick and was unable to finish. He pulled away and cursed me.

"What did you do to me?" he screamed. "*Puta*, what did you do to me?" He dressed, grabbed my arm, and pulled me down the stairs. "You cursed me!"

I knew without any doubt that God had once again intervened. I started to laugh, even though I was still high on coke. And that made it seem even funnier. Despite all the coke in my system, I'd had a conversation with God. As crazy as it may sound to write this, I knew it was true. God had delivered me once again. Just as Billy Graham had said, God would never leave me or give up on me—not now, not ever.

Paco yelled at Julio, "She's cursed!"

I marveled at what happened. I didn't go to church. I didn't read the Bible. The only time I prayed, it was something like, "God, don't let me get busted."

Why would God bother with me? Why wouldn't he give up like everyone else?

They don't care. They really don't care about us. We're

*nothing to them. It's all about the money. We are just dispos-
able commodities to them.*

Reality had set in. God was setting me free, even though
I didn't know what was going to happen next.

———☼———

Jan went to Marco's, and I went home and fell into a peace-
ful sleep. The next morning I got up, not knowing what to do
next. Those men know that with slaves like me there's what I
call an invisible chain—we are hooked and always want the
drugs. That dependency on a captor creates what is called
a trauma bond. These men had chosen us, hooked us, and
knew we would continue coming back to them.

It may be hard to understand that even though they were
mean to us and sold us to bad men who liked having sex with
children, they were also sweet and gave us food and coke.
Their kindness manipulated girls like me to believe the lies.
We told ourselves they would take care of us. This is what is
known as "Stockholm Syndrome."

At the time of this writing, people pay an average of $160
to $180 each time they have sex with a child. And the "boy-
friends" (pimps) get the majority of that. Most of the kids
who receive money never get the whole amount. I was never
offered money. They gave me only drugs, along with a false
sense of family, love, and belonging. Because I had nothing
to compare it with, I readily accepted their deception.

That's how they duped me. Because I was just a teenager
and never received money, I didn't believe I was part of a
prostitution ring. I never learned the truth until years later
that it was a crime for my body to be exchanged for drugs
and so-called love.

———☼———

The next day when I went back to Marco's apartment, I looked around and no one was there except Maria, a seventeen-year-old. Instead of greeting me, she said, "I heard you were with that guy Paco last night. Is that true?"

"Yes," I said. "Why?"

"You knew he has AIDS, didn't you?"

"No, I didn't," I said. "How do you know?"

"I was with him too and I'm getting tested. You'd better get tested."

As soon as her words sunk in, I said, "I forgot, I've got to go do something. Please don't tell them I was here, okay?"

I turned around and walked right out of that apartment.

At that time, there was a crazy belief that if a man with AIDS had sex with little girls, he could pass the virus on to them and be free of the disease. Paco was trying to get rid of his disease by infecting me and all of my young friends. Back then it was like a death sentence because there was no medicine to help anyone with AIDS.

But God spared me once again.

I went to our apartment. Mom was at work, so I went inside and locked the door, but my thoughts didn't stop. *That means they almost killed me. They knew Paco has AIDS and they didn't care. They didn't care that he was violent with me and raped me. They care only about the money.* At that moment, I wasn't high on drugs, and I clearly heard that word, *AIDS.*

They *knew,* and yet they didn't care.

When Mom came home, she could see that I was in bad shape. I was shaking and crying. I couldn't tell her everything, so I told Mom that Marco and his people were giving me drugs and that I wanted to stay away from those men. She already knew I was strung out on drugs.

"If those people from Marco's apartment come here," I pleaded, "tell them I'm not home." I was scared, remembering the threats they made at various times. I couldn't stop shaking as I talked to her. Because I was too ashamed, I couldn't tell her the whole truth.

Eventually I got tested for HIV, and when it came back negative, I knew God had saved me yet again. I promised God and myself there would never be another chance for that to happen.

I was going to get out. I didn't know how, but I knew I was going to get away. Drugs still controlled much of my thinking, but I sensed that somehow—soon—I would be free. God had spoken to me so many times, and I remembered those words: *I have a plan for you, and this is not it.*

And I still recalled the words Billy Graham said: "Remember this: God will never leave you or forsake you."

14

Almost Busted

After a night out, Jan and I stopped at the Eden Rock Hotel on Miami Beach the next morning. While I was with Paco, Jan had swiped more coke, and we snorted some of it in the public bathroom.

After that fix, we decided to walk on the beach. We were both fifteen years old. That was in 1987, and we were obviously young enough that anyone would have known we belonged in school in the middle of the day.

Just then, a police officer stopped us. "Shouldn't you two girls be in school?" he asked. "What are your names?"

The rule on the streets is never to give your real name, so I didn't. However, Jan was nervous, and without thinking she gave him her correct name. He called us over to his car and ran both names through the system. After waiting a few minutes, he said to Jan, "You're listed as a runaway."

We protested, but it did no good. "I have to take you in," he told Jan. He had nothing on me, so I was all right. Before the police officer took her away, Jan hugged me and slipped the coke into my shirt pocket.

The officer didn't hold me. If he had arrested me with possession of cocaine, it would have ruined my life. Because drug possession was a felony, I would have spent time in juvenile jail and had a criminal record, and I would not be where I am today.

He turned to me and asked, "Do you have a way home?"

"I have a car."

"You need to go home, little girl, because you should be in school."

"Yes, sir, no problem," I said as respectfully as I could. "I'll go home right now. I promise." And I meant those words.

"Dear God, please don't let me be arrested," I prayed earnestly. "If you help me not go to jail, I promise I will quit doing cocaine."

I intended to keep that promise.

———— ☼ ————

As soon as the police car was out of sight, I went back to my brother's Buick, which I had taken again without asking, and drove it home. When Mom came in from work, I told her, "Jan was arrested today. She's a runaway." By then Jan had been living with us for about nine months. I tried to make it sound like just an insignificant fact, but I felt anything but casual. I was still scared and realized how close I had come to being arrested.

I flushed the rest of the coke. I've never used cocaine since then.

———☼———

As I knew would happen, the traffickers came looking for me. Once we're "in," they think we belong to them. Most of the time they're right.

I didn't answer the door when they came. One evening, Mom was home when Marco came over asking for me.

"Kat is not going back to your apartment."

"We love her," Marco said. "She's part of our family too. We care—"

"You can't have her!" Mom cut him off in the middle of his sentence. "She's not going back. Not ever."

Marco smiled and walked away. I'm sure he didn't believe her. He knew how it worked. I was just beginning to learn that their talk about love and family was all part of the big setup. They never really loved us, they only wanted to use us and to make us rely on them for drugs.

The invisible chain would bring me back, or so Marco probably thought. There were spiritual forces at work, however, and Marco couldn't know that God had set me free.

Instead of returning to our apartment again himself, Marco sent girls. I refused to talk to them. At other times, the girls saw me on the street and tried to convince me to go back by saying, "Or you'll be in big trouble." I'd heard that before.

"You're a part of our group," they said most often. "We miss you and you've got to come with us." Usually they talked sweetly and told me how much they missed me.

"They almost made me get AIDS," I said. "I'm done with that."

They didn't give up. They still kept coming around or rushed up to me when they saw me on the street. We still lived in the same building as Marco, so it was hard to avoid all contact.

Marco and his group refused to quit trying, which was their mistake. Mom finally went to the manager of the building because she'd had enough. "There's an old man here in the building who gives drugs to little girls, and my daughter is one of them. Every day they're going in and out of his apartment." She demanded that he evict Marco.

Although the product of an abusive marriage herself, once Mom learned how they kept trying to get me back on drugs, she wasn't timid when it came to protecting her daughter. I'm not sure if she threatened to call the police, but Marco moved out that week.

Three weeks later, however, Marco was still sending girls after me. Two of them saw me on the street, ran up to me, and told me that Marco had been "kicked out of his nice apartment." I think they were trying to make me feel bad, but it didn't faze me.

"You want to know where he lives?" One of them smiled and added, "Marco always has coke, and he'll give you all you want."

"Marco misses you," the other girl said. "He loves you."

My addiction wasn't gone. I could feel my body tingling and demanding a fix. I didn't want to go, and yet that invisible chain started pulling me back. "Okay, I guess I can go once," I said.

I had just turned sixteen and now owned a white 1972 Toyota Corolla. I drove to Marco's new apartment. When I walked inside, I saw Beth. She was lying in bed with Marco.

Marco hugged me, and instead of letting me go, he began to fondle my breasts.

"I have something I need to do," I said and walked away. As I walked out of the building, I said—and meant—"I'm through with this. I'm through with these people. Forever."

I determined to break the invisible bondage. I saw what Beth had become. Marco was a sick man, something I finally admitted to myself. I no longer wanted their drugs or needed to hear their lies.

I got in my car and drove away from that building.

15

From Clubs to Gangs

had gotten free once again from those invisible chains that tried to keep me bound to abuse, drugs, and human trafficking, a life of misery and disrespect for myself.

I'm grateful to God that I never had to go into a rehab, which is unusual. God did a miracle for me. I prayed and the desire for cocaine left me. People who know the power of that addiction know that is a big, big deal. Few of us are able to kick the habit the way I did, but with God, all things are possible.

As I reviewed my life, I realized what a mess I had made of it. I was barely sixteen years old, a high school dropout, and had been lured into sex trafficking three times.

Jan, who had been my support system, was placed in foster care. I started reconnecting with former schoolmates by clubbing—that is, going to teen clubs. No one there used drugs, at least not that I saw. But they were into alcohol even though they couldn't buy it there. Before they went to one of the clubs, they'd find older people to buy booze for them. It wasn't long before I was part of that. Often we were drunk by the time we got to the clubs.

Running around with gangs who robbed and fought with other gangs became part of my lifestyle. Instead of trying to fit into what I would have called a hostile environment, I went where people would accept me. That was with gangs.

Then I met Al. He was part of the Thirty-Second Street Gang and hung around Miami in a rough part of town. One time I went to visit Al in his neighborhood. Another gang was having a problem with the Thirty-Second Street Gang, and they came toward us. It was obvious an altercation was going to take place and they would shoot at each other.

Just then, I heard the voice of God. I often wonder why the Lord would speak to me in such terrible places, even though I didn't listen.

But God spoke yet again—like a shout inside my head: *Walk across the street. Walk across the street and talk to those girls.*

That didn't make sense. I hardly knew them and couldn't think of anything to say, but the voice was so strong, I couldn't resist. In the past I'd heard and obeyed that inner voice, and it had always been right.

I started across. I had barely reached the curb when a car raced by. Gang members inside the car started firing at the group where I had been standing.

Al fell to the pavement. I ran back to him. Someone called 911 and they took him to the hospital.*

As I watched the ambulance take Al away, I said to myself,

---

*Al recovered from the gunshot wound, but I never saw him again.

"This is the end of my hanging around with gangs. If God hadn't told me to cross the street, I might have been hit as well. Maybe killed."

I soon found out Al had lots of girls, and I was just another one. He didn't really care about me. Once more, the truth was hard to take. I was being used again, and that was the end of my hanging around with gangs.

Realizing God had protected me from being shot and then learning about Al's other girls made it easy for me to leave.

As bad as I feel about that terrible lifestyle, I remind myself that God has used that experience and knowledge so I can help others by my understanding the dynamics of what those kids go through. I had been one of them—someone on the inside, unlike those on the outside who don't understand that dangerous, hate-filled, competitive environment.

I didn't go back to the gangs, but if I couldn't be with Al, the guy I thought I loved, what should I do? The depression became so bad, I again struggled with suicidal thoughts. *I'm no good; nobody really loves me. Who will miss me? Mom will be better off if I'm dead anyway.*

I told Mom that I wanted to commit suicide. I told her I had gone as far as trying to slit my wrists, but one nick of the razor blade was enough. I couldn't stand the blood, so I stopped. "I thought of taking four Tylenols to kill myself," I confessed. "I'm a mess and don't know what to do. I don't want to live anymore. Jan is gone, all my friends are gone, and I hate my life."

Going back to the old life wasn't an option, but where was the new way of life? Where could I find peace and some measure of happiness?

16

A Modeling Career

One evening I saw an ad on TV about a modeling school called John Casablancas Modeling and Career Center, and it was located in Miami.

I can do that. I can become a model.

After I told Mom about the ad, I asked, "Why don't you put me in modeling school? That will help me feel good about myself."

I still lived with a victim mentality. People lied to me and I believed them, so they took advantage of me. More slowly, my persona deteriorated to rebellion and anger because I was off drugs and had nothing to numb the pain of my life. I became fearful, compliant, and suffered from post-traumatic stress disorder (PTSD), severe depression, and low self-esteem.

I couldn't comprehend how people could always hurt me, not realizing that as an abuse and trafficking survivor I carried around an invisible target that showed predators how vulnerable I was. Once I was in a relationship, I was so afraid of abandonment that I did whatever anyone asked just to please them. I lost all sense of what I liked, needed, or wanted.

———— ☼ ————

At John Casablancas Modeling and Career Center, I made friends with the staff and with a few other students. Just being accepted there helped me to start feeling better and better about myself. Although there were girls there who asked me if I wanted to do coke, I declined and said I was trying hard to better my life. I really wanted to make my mom proud of me.

After I finished the course, I sought out modeling auditions and received several jobs. I was proud of myself. Twice I played an extra in the TV series *Miami Vice* that was filmed in Miami. That may not sound like a big deal, but it was special to me. I had found something I could do, and for someone like me to feel any level of success was big.

———— ☼ ————

I participated as a model in several boat shows around Miami and Fort Lauderdale. I wore bathing suits because having shapely, bathing-suit-clad women was supposed to help sell the boats. Besides, I was paid quite well.

To some, my modeling probably didn't sound like much, and I knew I would never be a top model, especially with my full figure. Although I was sexy and received compliments, I never seemed to be thin enough for the high-fashion modeling industry. Even so, I was happy and life was good.

God was somewhere in my life, but not as important as

he should have been. Even though I often heard his voice deep inside my heart and prayed regularly for guidance, I still held back.

God did protect me and I believe he orchestrated the positive things that were happening. Slowly he was helping me become who I was supposed to be.

I needed glasses, but I didn't like to wear them in public. I didn't consider contact lenses because of the inconvenience. And after I became a model, I felt eyeglasses detracted from the glamour of the profession.

Occasionally, I got together with Heidi, a girlfriend from elementary school. I suppose part of it was that I wanted to impress her by what I'd done with my life. On one occasion I drove Heidi and her boyfriend to Hialeah. She had the same problem as I did with poor eyesight, but we felt that wearing glasses made us look like nerds, so neither of us wore them.

After we dropped off Heidi's boyfriend, we were driving on Forty-Ninth Street in Hialeah when I thought I saw her former boyfriend. "Look there! That's Roger!" We pulled into a parking space and went back to talk to the group of guys who were there. I waved at Roger and he waved back.

But because of my nearsightedness, I was wrong. As I got closer and saw him, I realized he was a stranger. Although embarrassed, I started talking to him anyway.

His name was Joel and he was from Colombia, South America. Joel didn't speak much English and I didn't speak Spanish, but we spoke the universal language of love, and we were able to talk, laugh, and have fun together.

Soon we started dating. After I got to know Joel a little better, he told me about his dad, who was a drug dealer high up the chain in the Colombian cartel.

"That's cool," I said. Hearing about his father made Joel seem even more exciting. That was in 1988, when Colombians were known as "cocaine cowboys" because they ran drugs into the United States.

Joel was a hard worker at the local Winn-Dixie grocery store. He didn't do drugs, even though that was his father's business. If he had done drugs, I never would have dated him. I didn't want to be around a druggie. I was done with that.

After we started to date, I disconnected from my old friends. From here on, whatever I say about Joel is obviously my interpretation of our relationship. This phase of my life happened because I had just come out of a lifestyle in which I had few choices and was under the dominance of others. In retrospect, it seems natural that I would be attracted to a man like Joel.

I thought it was my decision, but looking back I have often wondered. It seems to me that like those who had snared me in the past, Joel isolated me from my family and friends. He took me to his family functions, and I acquiesced because I wanted to please him. I liked his parents, especially his dad because he had a sense of humor.

I was still modeling and had enrolled in night school, where I received praise for my work. I also went to work as a secretary in my dad's office because I didn't have modeling gigs every day. My new lifestyle built up my self-esteem.

My life was going smoothly. Joel and I were dating, and our relationship was becoming serious. Mom liked Joel and said he was a normal man, not involved in gangs and not into drugs. We didn't tell her that Joel's father was in the Colombian cartel.

———— ✿ ————

I entered the Miss Teen USA Pageant. I had gotten sponsors, people who paid money for me to go into the pageant. My life was changing. I felt so good about myself. It felt awesome to be off drugs and away from those bad people. I was happy, beautiful, young, and getting stronger on my way toward a successful future.

Soon the sponsors wanted me to consider going into the Miss USA Pageant. I was excited. My path was coming together and life would be wonderful. Since I had worked for my dad off and on over the years, I knew a great deal about business and began learning how to start new businesses and how to get listings and sell real estate. Everything seemed perfect.

———— ✿ ————

I fell in love with Joel—and that's not surprising to me now. He showed me attention and affection, and I believed it was genuine. He treated me nicely, and I assumed that eventually we'd be married.

I didn't really want to have sex with him. When we met, I was trying to be good, and I was determined that I was going to wait until we were married. That was my chance to start over. More than once I told him, "I'm not ready for anything more."

Joel persisted. "I love you," he said many times.

Not only did I like hearing those words, I needed to hear them from someone other than people involved in sex trafficking.

After three months, I gave in to Joel's insistence. After

we finished, I started crying. I wasn't on drugs. Until then I hadn't been doing anything I thought was bad, but the pain from the past abuse hit me.

Oh, dear God, I've failed you again, and I've failed myself.

The sex continued. One day I suspected I was pregnant with Joel's child, but I didn't want to say anything to anyone. Instead, I visited a women's clinic around the corner from our apartment. They gave pregnancy tests for five dollars. The woman in charge confirmed my suspicions. I felt terrible and unsure of what to do.

"It's your right to have an abortion, you know." She kept talking about my legal rights.

"What about the baby?" I asked. "Will the baby be hurt? Will he feel anything?"

"No, it's not even a baby," she insisted. "It's a blob of tissue." She persisted, "You're still a beautiful young girl and you don't need to throw your life away like that. Just wait there. You need to speak with the doctor. She is in and can do the abortion today."

"I guess I could talk to the doctor." There was my compliance again, and it was the only way I knew to stop her from pressuring me.

Leave. Get up and leave this place.

Without the slightest doubt, I knew God had spoken, and I had to leave. Not speaking to anyone, I got up and walked out of the women's clinic.

As I walked around the corner to where we lived, God definitely spoke to me: *I love this child, and I have a plan for this child's life.*

"What should I do, God? What about *my* life? I've finally gotten my life back together."

I have a plan for this baby.

I just kept hearing those words inside my head. As I walked home, my brother, Daniel, was the first person I saw. The words burst out, even though I hadn't meant to say anything: "I'm pregnant."

We hadn't been close in a long time, and I expected an angry reaction. Instead, Daniel gave me a strong hug. "Don't worry, Kat, I'm going to help you take care of this baby. And this baby is going to be a surfer like me. I'm going to help you and be there for him, I promise."

My brother will never know how wonderful the embrace and the words were to me. I felt God had given me a sign—proof—that I was to have the baby.*

When I told Joel I was pregnant, he didn't seem surprised. That made me suspect that he had gotten me pregnant on purpose.

Even though God had spoken to me and I knew I had made the right decision, I still struggled. *This is going to ruin my life. I've tried so hard to do well and get my life straight.*

I knew what I had to do next. Immediately, I went to an official of the Miss Teen USA Pageant and told her about my pregnancy.

"You have to drop out of the pageant," the leader said. "A pregnant teen is not a role model."

I hated hearing those words, but she was right. In 1989, pregnant teens were shunned in society much more than they are today.

*Daniel never went back on his word. My son is now in his early twenties, and his uncle has been like a hero and a second father to him.

"You've messed up your life," Mom said. She was right, and that made me feel even worse. I had once again brought shame on myself and my family. I had tried so hard to be good, and now I was embarrassing my mother. She had an unmarried, pregnant teen for a daughter.

"I did this to myself," I said many times. "I got myself into this." Being pregnant, I could no longer model, so there went my career.

Shortly after that, Joel and I met with Joel's mother and her friends one evening. The meeting lasted until four o'clock in the morning. They pressured us to get married. "You have to give this child a father."

Joel proposed, probably because of their pressure. Although I didn't want to marry him, I felt obligated. I wanted to give my baby a wholesome family life. Because I was seventeen years old and still a minor, I had to get my parents' permission. Both Mom and Dad agreed it was the right thing to do. A justice of the peace married us.

Ashamed and embarrassed, I went through the brief ceremony. This was one of the saddest days of my life. Several times I felt like crying; instead, I forced a smile on my face.

———☼———

Joel's mother had insisted that we marry, but I felt she had more in mind than providing a legal father for the baby. She wanted her legal citizenship too, and through our marriage both she and Joel eventually received that.

Although I have no way of knowing Joel's heart, I can say that he professed faith in Jesus Christ and put on a show for his mother during our marriage, but I'm not sure he ever had a spiritual change. He went to church with me, and everyone accepted him. Joel was likable, and he smiled and chatted with everyone and seemed sincere. But once we were home, he behaved differently. I saw no real evidence of God in his life outside the church building.

———— ☼ ————

Even though I was a pregnant teen and shunned by society, God was still with me. I had been going to night school, and in my sixth month of pregnancy I dropped out.

About the time I dropped out of school, I learned that my history teacher had nominated me for "Outstanding High School Students of America" and "Who's Who Among American High School Students." I received both awards, and that boosted my confidence in my ability to learn. So I studied and earned my high school diploma through a GED.

A month after my eighteenth birthday, in February 1990, I gave birth to our son, whom we nicknamed Kipper. Even before Kipper's birth, I had disconnected from my friends, and they turned their backs on me too. They didn't come out and say, "You're a pregnant teen," but the attitude was obvious.

My son was one month old the Sunday morning the pastor gave an altar call for people to turn to Christ or to rededicate their lives to Jesus. I had made that initial commitment as a child. Even though God protected me, I hadn't been faithful. Many times I'd pondered God's mercy in saving me from terrible situations when I hadn't followed him. Yet God never gave up on me. And the words that Billy Graham had said rang true once more: "God will never leave you or forsake you."

"I'm going forward," I told Joel. "Do you want to go with me?"

And just like my dad, who years before had stayed in the stands, Joel stayed where he was.

I went anyway. By the time I reached the front, I was crying and couldn't stop. In that moment, I realized I had tried to give up control of my life but felt ashamed for failing God so miserably. "God, take me back," I pleaded. "I don't want to be in control of my life anymore."

God did a marvelous work in my life. Many times after that I failed, but from that moment on, I wanted God as the center of my life.

After that Sunday morning at the altar, I wanted to become a true follower. Part of that determination came about because of Kipper. I determined to raise my son to believe in God. My life had been so crazy, and I didn't want him to go through that kind of turmoil.

Many times I've told Kipper that God used him to bring me back to himself. Until my son was born, I tried to be good on my own, yet I hadn't fully surrendered to God. I didn't go to church or pray. But God was faithful. He had told me that he had a plan not only for my life but for my baby's life as well. Because of Kipper, I was finally able to hear and act on that. God was leading me in the right way.

That day I threw myself on the altar and rededicated my life to him. I know only that after that morning, my life was never the same. I had finally surrendered everything, and God had taken me back. It would still take a long time for me to follow completely, but I had started down the pathway. And as a result of giving my life back to Christ, my mom and brother began witnessing the change. After a while, they too surrendered to Jesus Christ.

17

Wedded Bliss?

earned my GED just before the birth of our son. After that, my brother encouraged me to enroll in a community college and I did. I took classes at night and worked full-time during the day.

Because of my work for Dad, I already knew as much about the real estate business as most people ever learn. Dad, Mom, Daniel, and I were all in the real estate business. My brother earned his license shortly after his eighteenth birthday. Until I turned eighteen, however, I couldn't apply for a license. So after my eighteenth birthday, I took the examination and passed without any difficulty. Until then I didn't have any idea that I was really smart, because most of the people in my life were negative and told me how stupid I was. I believed them.

We moved with my mom to Bay Harbor, a nice, upscale

neighborhood. During the first years of their marriage, when my parents had been millionaires, they had owned a mansion in Golden Beach. I was born into a family with money. But after the divorce, my dad took everything. He still had the money, but we didn't see much of it.

As I often think about it, everything I have in life I had to learn to get all on my own—and with God's help. At age nineteen, Joel and I bought our first home. I looked into financing and proved that we could pay the mortgage, so the bank gave us a loan.

I enjoyed working in real estate, but ever since I was a kid, I had wanted to be a lawyer, so law school was the obvious next step. I felt I could help other kids; I wanted to be there for them because no one had been there to help me.

About a year after Kipper's birth, we were living with my mother. Joel wanted us to move to Hialeah, where his family lived. I agreed because it was time for us to move out and be on our own. It hadn't been a good living arrangement with the three of us living with Mom and my brother in a one-bedroom apartment.

Joel stopped working at Winn-Dixie and found a job with a moving company, which paid better. Later, he began to install garage doors. His mother went back to Colombia, but she couldn't afford to stay there, so we paid for her to come back to Florida. In return, she would take care of our son while I worked.

That was a big mistake.

———— ☼ ————

There always seemed to be conflict between Joel and me. I don't want to lay all the blame on him. Neither of us came from healthy backgrounds, so it was probably inevitable. When our son was only two years old, Joel and I separated because of what I called his intense jealousy. "You never want me to be free to do things on my own," I said, not realizing that in his culture wives were submissive to their husbands.

We finally reconciled and, to Joel's credit, he let me go out with my friends—friends from my old life. Those old friends tried pulling me back into their lifestyle of drinking and smoking pot. I resisted, but they pleaded, "Come out on the weekends. You work hard all week."

As a result of my so-called freedom, Joel and I fought over little things that often grew into big things.

Old friends from middle school kept pulling me back and telling me I was missing the fun in life. They insisted I was too young to be tied down, and I agreed with them. Outside of our church, they were the only friends I had. But the best thing was that I could always be myself around them.

Joel and I came from different cultures. I was an American and so were my friends. His friends spoke only Spanish. His mother knew almost no English and didn't try to learn. Because she took care of my son all day and didn't speak any English, naturally she taught him to speak only in Spanish. I was resentful because at times I couldn't communicate with him.

Whenever I went to see Joel's family, the tension was terrible and, whether it was intentional or not, I always felt left out of their conversation. I had stopped smoking before my son was born, but I took it up again as well as drinking and cursing. I felt so bad about my life that I didn't care what they thought of me.

The situation worsened. His mother moved in with us, and

she took over our house. She rearranged the furniture and brought in their Colombian friends. On almost any night, we'd have several people sleeping in our home, eating our food, and using our laundry facilities. Joel's sister brought her son over for free babysitting, but by now we were paying his mother to take care of our son.

At first I was the timid, submissive wife. I didn't say anything, but the resentment built. One day I exploded and yelled at his mother and sister. "You need to leave! You have to get out of my house!"

When Joel came home from work, he angrily shouted at me, "You did that to my mother and my sister?" In his Latin culture, if I disrespected his parents, I brought shame on him. "I'm embarrassed," he said repeatedly. "I can't believe what you did."

"I won't take this anymore," I said, and meant it.

"Then leave the house. Get out, Kat!"

That was the end of the argument. I took my son and left. I went back to live with my mother.

After I left Joel, I decided to get a divorce, even though I didn't want one and didn't feel it was right. The main reason I gave in to the pressure to marry him was to have a father for our son, and I hadn't wanted my son to grow up in a single-parent home.

While separated, I went out drinking with my friends and got really drunk one night, and it made me sick. I suffered from a terrible hangover—worse than anything I'd ever had. My mom encouraged me to go back home to Joel and, sick as I was, I called him. He let me come home.

Joel was very nice to me, didn't fight with me, and took care of me until I was better. Maybe, I thought, we could make this marriage work. The following Sunday we went to church and heard a message on marriage and reconciliation. I went forward, and this time Joel went with me. Both of us rededicated our lives and our family to the Lord. In 1991, Joel and I were baptized in that church.

After that, Joel spoke to his mother and set boundaries. She moved out and went to live with his sister. Her move didn't resolve all the issues, and he still spent a lot of time with them, but life was better—for a while. Both women still had a lot of influence over him, and that may have been part of his culture.

After rededicating my life to God, I enrolled as a student at Trinity International University in Davie, Florida. Before long, I also started working there. The job came about because on one of their radio programs, they spoke about jobs at the university. I called the station to see if they had any jobs I could apply for. I wanted to get a better job, and it would be an opportunity to get away from my controlling father.

The radio host sent me to talk to Bee Justamante, who was friendly and warm, and after a single interview, she hired me. I later got to know a godly man and father figure, Dr. Stefan Tchividjian, who also worked there. His was the radio voice that had sent me to Trinity. Later I learned that Dr. Tchividjian was Billy Graham's son-in-law.

I was grateful to God. By then I was twenty-four years old, working and going to school in a Christian environment—so different from anything I'd known before. At first I coordinated classes for Excel, which is an accelerated degree program, and then I went to work for the development department where I got to know Dr. T (as we affectionately called him).

One day I spoke with Dr. T's wife, Gigi Tchividjian, who was Billy Graham's daughter. On the phone I clearly sensed the presence of God in her voice, especially when she told me about raising her large family. I smiled as I thought about the influence of the Graham family in my life.

My job at Trinity University included coordinating the manuals and classes for the adult education program. The development department promoted me to assistant to the director, where I coordinated Christian women's events and fund-raiser dinners. That gave me the opportunity to meet many well-known Christians, such as Dr. Tony Evans, Pastor Steve Brown, Luis Palau, Evelyn Christiansen, and other famous authors and speakers.

After that, I moved over to Trinity's radio station, WMCU, and I helped set up their big events. I met many influential people who really took the time to pour their interest into my life.

Steve James ran the radio station, and he told me about his church in Fort Lauderdale. In 1996, when our church went through a split, Joel and I decided to visit Steve's church. We liked it and became regular attendees there.

Educationally, the difference between Joel and me widened. I had passed my GED and gone on to college, but Joel had never graduated from high school. I kept advancing, and because of my good grades in college, I received scholarships and awards for my accomplishments.

My acceptance by the Christian community increased and

my self-esteem grew. I made top grades, which surprised me because I hadn't been a good student as a kid. "Who would have known I would do well in school when I wasn't forced to go?" I told my mom.

The new me—the real me—was beginning to emerge. While I was still an undergraduate student, I met Diane Johnson, a professor at Trinity. She was a wonderful example to me of a godly woman, and she discipled me and taught me many things. And in 1995, when our second child was born, we named her Diana, in honor of Diane. That same year I graduated cum laude (with honors) from Trinity International University with a Bachelor of Arts degree in Human Resources Management. I was the first one in my family to receive a college degree.

Because I had earned my bachelor's degree, I could take the next step in my desire to help others. I still wanted to go to law school; however, that didn't happen right away. Instead, I resigned my position at the radio station in 1997 to become a stay-at-home mother. The major reason I quit was because the pastor of our church regularly preached against mothers working. "You don't want your kid raised in day care," was one of his regular messages. I felt all right about staying at home to raise my children in the Lord. But financially it was difficult for us living only on Joel's income.

I took my dad and Joel's younger brother, Julian, to a play called *Heaven's Gates and Hell's Flames*. They both went forward and received Christ. To finally see my father turn to Jesus Christ was one of the happiest moments of my life.

Mom had been influential in my dad's turning to God because she stayed in his life and was a consistent example of God's love in spite of all the years of abuse. Even though they were divorced, when Dad became seriously ill, Mom went to live with him and take care of him. It was through her consistent love and our prayers that my father's heart and life finally turned toward Christ, and he was ready to make a public confession when I took him to the play.

——— ☼ ———

One day I felt convicted to tell Julian, "You're staying out every night until eleven or twelve o'clock, and that is a terrible example to Kipper." He had been living with us for nearly five years. He didn't seem to want to change, so I finally said, "It's time for you to find another place to live."

I knew Joel wouldn't tell Julian that, because he felt responsible for him. I was most upset because Julian went to his stepsister's house every weekend. The woman was a lesbian, and her girlfriend was involved in Santeria, a religion that is a mixture of African and Caribbean witchcraft and Roman Catholicism. Each time Julian spent time with them, he came back antagonistic and argumentative because the other woman was jealous of Julian's relationship to his sister.

Joel and I prayed regularly for all three of them. Finally, the other woman demanded that the sister choose between her and Julian. The sister chose Julian and her relationship with the other woman ended.

A few weeks after that, Julian's sister came to our house. "I know you've been praying for me. Thank you," she said. "I'm not in that lifestyle anymore." Not long after that, she met a man online, they fell in love, and they were married.

Seeing God use that was a huge encouragement, even though my husband had become angry when I told his brother to leave. Although I knew it had been the right thing to do, it caused a lot of friction between Joel and me.

———— ☼ ————

After Julian moved out, there were only four of us—Joel, me, and our two children. By then Kipper had started school and I was home with our baby daughter. One day God spoke to me about helping Joel start his own business. It seemed so obvious, I wondered why I hadn't done that earlier. That day I had what I can only describe as a vision. Inside my head I saw Joel as a boss with other men working for him. I knew it was from God and that it would happen. I had faith that God could do anything.

I prayed fervently for guidance. Joel was good with his hands and liked working with a friend installing garage doors. Joel caught on quickly and was very good at his work.

I continued to pray daily for guidance because I wanted to be sure I had heard from the Lord. After a few more days, I thought that with the skills Joel had developed it seemed natural for him to start his own garage door business.

I decided to tell Joel what God had impressed on my heart. "God is telling me that I need to help you start your own business."

"We can't do that. I wouldn't have a regular paycheck." He had never done anything so risky, and I understood his resistance. I also knew that with God's help, we could do it.

"It will work. And I'm going to help you get those accounts." I told him that I had been praying and what God had shown me. "I'm going to help you set it up, and I'll also help you get accounts with major companies. You'll become a boss and have workers under you."

I sensed he was scared that he wouldn't make enough money to provide for us. I understood his feelings. I also had faith that what God had said, God would do.

We started the business. I kept the books and taught Joel how to attract customers. Our next step was to attract big accounts. I went to Home Depot and asked them to list us as one of their subcontractors. They gave me forms, which I took home, filled out, and brought back.

The manager read the forms, shook his head, and said, "We've never had anyone do an application so well. Even though you've only been in business for two months, we're going to give you this contract. Usually we don't do that for anyone who has been in business less than two years."

That happened in 1999; Joel still has his subcontractor account with Home Depot.

18

Learning about Boundaries

The stress of a new business, financial pressure, and our working together created a lot of tension. It seemed like Joel took out his anxieties and frustrations on me. That led to pushing and shoving—and I sensed it was slowly escalating. Nothing I said or did seemed to please Joel. Because of abuse in my background, I didn't fret too much about his attitude and behavior. I didn't like it, but I accepted that as the way life worked.

In 2000, we started going to a small church in Miami Lakes. Almost from the beginning, I observed the relationship between the pastors and their wives. I never saw any evidence of yelling or pushing. They treated each other with respect, which seemed strange to me. Maybe it had been the same at other churches, but I hadn't noticed. Now I did.

Not long afterward, I began attending a Bible counseling

class at the larger mother church in Fort Lauderdale. One week the lesson was about abuse—all kinds of mistreatment.

The teacher pointed out the characteristics of domestic abuse.

That's what I'm living in.

That's when I began to realize that things weren't okay. Many, many nights I cried myself to sleep. I was in pain but I didn't know why. I hadn't been able to give a name to what troubled me. But when I opened up to him, Pastor John said, "If you're living in a bad situation, that's not okay."

For the first time I felt someone understood.

In that class I could hardly believe what I heard. I hadn't known what I'd experienced was abuse, even when it came to our sexual relationship. Sometimes I didn't feel like having sex, and despite my saying no, Joel forced me. I later found out that where verbal abuse exists, there is often sexual abuse and rape in marriage. Today we call that marital rape.

By then we had been married eleven years and our relationship never improved after that. I told Joel that I wanted him to see a counselor, but he refused and my self-esteem started to dip.

Probably because of my persistence, Joel finally agreed for us to see a counselor at the larger church. In our first meeting, I told the counselor about several episodes, such as how angry Joel had gotten when I gave a needy boy a pair of sneakers and how Joel had verbally abused me in front of our kids. Joel told him what a terrible mother I was because I spent eleven dollars on a pair of shoes that I gave away. Then I related instances when Joel pushed me, slammed doors, and yelled in anger.

The counselor listened and finally told me, "You're not

submitting to your husband. That's the reason this is happening to you." He quoted 1 Peter 3:5, which commands women to submit to their husbands, but he never said anything about the husband loving his wife, as in Ephesians 5:25. That male counselor didn't seem to care about Joel's attitude or behavior, and he frequently ignored my responses and insisted that I needed to submit.

I was crushed. I had finally gone for help and been knocked down. I felt the church had let me down, and I felt even more condemned. I didn't know what was wrong with me or why I deserved such treatment. Because of that meeting, Joel seemed to act as if the counselor had given him permission to continue doing as he pleased.

I write this because I want abuse within marriage to come to an end. For many years I didn't even know there was a law against being raped in my own bed.

I didn't know any better, so I lived with the situation. The abuse worsened. One time Joel accused me of adultery because I was helping one of the pastors at the church. I only wanted to serve God and to help needy people, and I needed to feel I belonged somewhere. By then I had become a shell of the person that I was before.

People who had known me before I got married realized I had changed. I lost my spontaneity, drive, and extroverted personality and became extremely submissive, shy, and introverted. As a result of constant intimidation, I was afraid to speak up about anything.

I prayed and reminded myself that God was faithful. Many times I thought, *There must be somebody in church who understands.* I had devoted my life to God and yet, because I was constantly being hammered down, I had no joy or peace in my life. *When I'm in such a terrible, painful home situation, how can I serve God?*

"I want to be a godly woman who pleases you in every way," I prayed daily. "I don't know how to do that when I'm being told I'm worthless and useless." I remembered the terrible life God had delivered me from and realized that as bad as my marriage was, life was better than it had been before. But I was still miserable.

I lost weight to look good for Joel, but he accused me of having an affair. Nothing I did seemed to please him. I became sad and depressed and didn't know what to do.

Unable to take any more stress, I became so physically sick I lay in bed for a full week. My head was killing me and I ached everywhere. Finally, I made an appointment with a doctor and Joel went with me, which he'd never done before. Looking back, I believe God wanted him there so he could hear the doctor say that I needed to go to a neurologist.

A woman in our church worked for a neurologist, and she got us in the next day. She was such a busy woman, it was a miracle to get in that quickly.

Again, Joel went with me. After the doctor examined me, she turned to my husband. "If you don't cut some of the tension out of your wife's life, she's going to die. She's under so much stress that it's adversely affecting her body."

The doctor put me on medication to cut down the stress. I continued to cry out to God to help me—not just to be free from tension, but to change my life and make me happy.

About that time I bought several CDs by Dr. Charles Stanley, pastor of Atlanta's First Baptist Church, whom I had watched and enjoyed on TV. As I listened to the CDs, God seemed to whisper that I needed to get in touch with that church and they would be able to help me.

On the back of each CD cover was the ministry's contact information. I called and spent more than an hour on the phone with a female counselor. She was compassionate and kind and listened to me pour out my pain. As a result, the woman asked for my address and sent me a large stack of books.

The woman from Dr. Stanley's church also referred me to a wonderful counselor, Marsha Medders, who had an office at First Baptist Church of Fort Lauderdale. She was truly a godsend and met with me and Joel for three months. At first she met with us together, then separately so she could work with us individually. Because she was nonthreatening, Joel kept going—I think to please me so I wouldn't leave him.

At one meeting Marsha said to him, "You need to stop abusing your wife—verbally and physically. Stop pushing her and begin respecting your wife."

After that session, he told me he was finished with counseling. He would not be going again and said I couldn't either because he wouldn't pay for it.

I don't recall what I said, but I prayed a great deal after that. Again, God answered my prayer. I still held a real estate license, and a couple from the church in Miami Lakes told me, "We want to buy a house, and we want you to be our real estate agent."

Everything worked out, and within two months they moved into their new house and I had the money to pay for the rest of my counseling.

Joel probably sensed that I was changing, because his old methods no longer worked. One fear kept hitting me: if I left my husband I would have to live alone, and I'd never lived alone. I poured out my heart in an email to the senior pastor at the big church. I was still unsure of myself, and those tormenting voices from my past kept telling me I was bad. Whenever I had tried to defend myself to Joel, he always insisted that I was the one in the wrong. I was also afraid that my husband might hit me in the face. Even though I didn't have any broken bones, I had been bruised and injured both internally and externally many times.

For thirteen years I had minimized the abuse. No one was aware of how bad it truly was because it took place behind closed doors. My kids were aware only of his verbal abuse, although that affected them as well.

The pastor emailed, "Please visit our women's ministry. See Peggy Banks." Peggy led the women's ministry in that church. Later, she earned her doctorate writing on human trafficking and its spiritual effects.

I visited her office, and when I told her about our marriage, she looked right into my eyes and said, "That is abuse." Then she added, "You don't need to take it. There are laws to protect you and your children. You need to file a police report. The police will be on your side."*

That was the first time I had heard there were laws to protect *me*. I wanted to learn more.

---

*Later we worked together because we had so much in common. Peggy Banks is now with an anti-trafficking organization to free sex slaves.

19

Lessons from Law School

n 2004, I took a job as a loan officer at SunTrust Bank. The following year I did a presentation at St. Thomas University, located in Miami. We went there to present banking options to the employees and to offer our services.

Classes had gotten out early for spring break, so on the day of our appointment not many people attended. Since I had long wanted to go to law school, when we finished our presentation I decided to walk around the campus and find out more about their program.

I met Dr. Roza Pati, who told me about their Master of Law (LLM) program in Intercultural Human Rights. The program was designed for lawyers who wanted to specialize in this area of international law.

God used something as simple as the school's timing for spring break to allow me to investigate the program. Dr. Pati and I took to each other immediately, and she became my first mentor in anti–human trafficking work.*

At the time we met, however, I had no idea who she was or how much she knew about human trafficking. I also didn't realize that meeting with her was my first interview to gain entrance into their program.

We started talking, and she was very open with me and talked as if she had already accepted me as a student. "In this program you'll learn all about human trafficking," she said to me. "You'll learn about child soldiering. About domestic violence." When she started telling me the specific things, especially domestic violence and human trafficking, I was shocked, and I *knew* that I had to attend.

"What is human trafficking?" I asked.

"That's when people are bought and sold and used for purposes that they're not intended for and that they don't want to do. It's slavery."

Although I didn't tell her, I thought, *That's me!* But I kept silent about most of my experiences; I wasn't secure enough to divulge everything of my past at that time. It would take years of studying there before I finally opened up.

Roza answered all my questions about the program, and she was sweet and gentle. She gave me a packet for prospective students. I took it home and filled it out. She later contacted me and wanted to meet with me and introduce me to the founder of the program, Professor Siegfried Wiessner. He would become one of my biggest supporters in moving beyond my abuse. The staff was composed of international

*Later, Pope Benedict XVI appointed Dr. Roza Pati to be a member of the Pontifical Council for Justice and Peace at the Vatican. She is now one of the top international experts in the field.

experts who were writing textbooks and speaking for human rights around the world. Best of all, they were some of the kindest and warmest people I'd ever met.

When Roza officially interviewed me, she told me that everybody in the class was a lawyer. "And your coming in will be an exception."

They are willing to make an exception for me?

I could hardly believe what I heard. I had my undergraduate degree, but I still felt inadequate. As I listened to her, I thought, *God brought me here.*

As part of my pre-enrollment, I spoke with Professor Wiessner, and we talked about my background. He handed me a fifty-page pamphlet he had written. "Take this with you and write me a ten-page paper on it. I'd like to have it by midnight Sunday." That happened Friday afternoon.

The following Thursday I received my acceptance letter.

Tears came to my eyes when I read it. God had done another miracle for me. My acceptance—as an exceptional student—told me that God had overcome the obstacles for me and that I belonged at St. Thomas.

As I expected, Joel resisted my returning for further education. He always had a reason, the most common being, "That's going to take your time away from the family."

After several talks, we reached an understanding. I would study only after everyone was asleep so it wouldn't interfere with family time.

I had to pray and discern the right path. Was it God's will for me? If I went to school, was I being a biblically submissive wife? The more I prayed, the more positive I was that God had opened a door of service for me and I was to go forward.

I went back to Professor Wiessner and Roza and explained that I was a mother of two children and I also worked. To my delight, they were willing to allow me to attend part-time (another exception). They understood my situation, and being true human rights activists, they encouraged me and helped me once again.

When I got home, I could hardly wait to tell my husband about my day.

"I don't want to hear about it." He left the room and slammed the door. He came out demanding I perform sexually and threatened to cancel our upcoming vacation if I didn't.

I cried because I wanted to share my heart with him. My first day of law school had been wonderful. Even though I wasn't going to be a lawyer, I was excited. God had brought me to the school for a purpose, and with that education I could make a difference in the lives of other hurting people.

Money for the program was a problem. SunTrust, the bank where I worked, paid a third of my tuition—and I've always been grateful.

Roza frequently encouraged me. One day she asked, "Why don't you apply for the Intercultural Law Review?" She was on the board, so I put in my application. I appeared in front of all my professors and other dignitaries. They asked questions and I shared a little of my background. I was cautious and focused on the domestic abuse. I wasn't ready to come out and tell everything.

They accepted me as a member of the St. Thomas Intercultural Human Rights Law Review on Human Trafficking in 2005–2006. The law review was reserved for exceptional students to research and analyze articles submitted for publication in their prestigious journal of collective works by experts in their field.

While I was at St. Thomas, I met a professor who would also change my life for the better, Dr. Rev. Raul Fernandez-Calienes. I met him when my paper for the Women Moving Forward International Conference was accepted for a panel discussion. I had gotten several of the international leaders together and we wrote about our personal stories of women's advancement. Those stories were later published in a book.

I also wrote an article on domestic violence for the online publication of the International Museum of Women. I used part of my own story. That was the first time I had anything published, and it boosted my sense of self-value. After that, I had the privilege of writing a chapter in volume 2 of a book titled *Women Moving Forward*, which depicted women overcoming obstacles. I wasn't ready to write all of my personal story, so I wrote the story of my mother coming from Finland and how it impacted me. I used that story to compare women's human rights in the United States to those in Europe.

During that time I was working on my master's thesis, "Advancing a Better Quality of Life for Women and Children within the Church: Overcoming Domestic Violence in the Christian Society."

The following year I was again on the law review, and the topic was child soldiering. I read many terrible accounts about children in war-torn countries. Usually the child soldiers were only about ten years old when they received a machine gun and a machete and were forced to kill.

I finally met a young man who had been a child soldier. He became my good friend, and I love him dearly. He explained that they were thrown into combat as soldiers, which is a form of human trafficking. Many of them were also drugged and used for sexual purposes.

———✧———

St. Thomas had what is called *The Bluebook*, and I studied it thoroughly because that book contained everything I
needed to know in the legal field. I felt as if I were learning a
second language, but I stayed with it so I would be proficient
enough to write and review those papers.

We reviewed articles sent to us to make sure they lined up
with the *Bluebook* writing standard for legal papers. After
we validated the pieces, we made a compilation of the articles
for publication.

We studied other international human rights cases of torture, war crimes, genocide, crimes against humanity, child soldiering, trafficking, and domestic violence. During my studies,
I became educated on the laws pertaining to women's human
rights. One such law really stood out for me, "The Right to
Dignity," Article 3, which states, "Every woman shall have the
right to dignity inherent in a human being and to the recogni-
tion and protection of her human and legal rights. . . . [This
includes] respect for her dignity and protection of women from
all forms of violence, particularly sexual and verbal violence."
This statement appeared in the *Protocol to the African Charter
on Human and Peoples' Rights on the Rights of Women in
Africa*. I read the words from the charter: "Every woman shall
be entitled to respect for her life and the integrity and security
of her person. All forms of exploitation, cruel, inhuman and
degrading punishment and treatment shall be prohibited."*

*African Commission on Human and Peoples' Rights, *Protocol to the African
Charter on Human and Peoples' Rights on the Rights of Women in Africa*, adopted
by the 2nd Ordinary Session of the Assembly of the Union, Maputo, Mozambique,
July 11, 2003; http://www.achpr.org/instruments/women-protocol/#3.

As I read those words, they made sense to me—and for my own life. If women in Africa were permitted to live free from violence and exploitation, why wasn't I? I knew then that God had brought me to hear these words and gain strength from my sisters across the globe. I longed to be delivered from violence and oppression, even within my own home.

I did not have to take the abuse any longer.

———☼———

As part of my graduation requirements, I presented a 110-page thesis. As I wrote words about freedom from bondage, I was being healed. At times the pain had been so severe, I had to stop and wipe away tears. I did the research with other women in mind, but I was reaping the primary benefit.

I put my thesis to practical use by starting a Bible study for women who were experiencing abuse. I had sought answers from the church on this issue, but now I saw that God could use me and my experiences to help others.

At Women in Distress, a domestic violence shelter, I had taken classes on abuse in marriage and had even helped a classmate who moved to the shelter because she was being abused. She heard that I was writing on domestic violence, asked for help, and came to my Bible study. Several other women from the shelter came to the study for healing.

My mother also attended and openly faced her abuse. I knew some of it, but I had no idea how impactful that would be for me and for her. As I learned to set boundaries, I was able to help my mother set hers. I also needed to teach my daughter the lessons so I wouldn't pass down the message that abuse is acceptable. In helping others, I was also helping Mom and myself deal with past pain.

———☼———

I graduated from St. Thomas Law School in 2007. That graduation day, God made me feel special, and I knew he had chosen me for his service.

While completing my LLM thesis on domestic violence in the church, I received a major shock: none of the local churches I surveyed had a program devoted to domestic violence, let alone a human trafficking ministry. (Domestic violence and human trafficking often run in the same circles.)

I took the next step, and in 2008, I enrolled in a PhD program at Nova Southeastern University in Fort Lauderdale.

My dissertation was on the vulnerability factors and lures used to recruit American kids into trafficking.

———☼———

At Nova, they had a Biggest Loser program, and I lost fifty pounds. I felt good about myself and my self-esteem shot up. My husband, however, didn't like it. "Now other men are going to look at you," he said. By then his responses no longer surprised me.

The year I enrolled at Nova, I stopped working at the bank because the real estate market took a downturn. My husband asked, "Why don't you come back to work for me?" Reluctantly, I agreed. I thought that working for him again might give us a chance to grow closer. Things should have been good between us. However, shortly after I went back to work for him the abusive behavior started all over.

This time something woke me up and helped me to make a decision.

20

Making the Break

As my daughter and I climbed into the car to run an errand, Joel began to verbally abuse me—right in front of her. I tried desperately to appease him, but nothing worked.

As we drove away, my daughter asked, "Why are you shaking?" I don't remember how I answered, but that's when I realized a significant fact: I could never be happy with Joel. Not ever. Something I did or said always upset him. Besides that, I felt he never celebrated anything I did; rather, he used my achievements to put me down.

Why do I continue to put up with it?

———✦———

About two weeks later, I volunteered to co-lead a weeklong summer camp trip for middle schoolers. My daughter went to the camp with me.

When my co-leader and I were alone, she confessed she was in an abusive marriage. After we talked about it, she said, "You've opened my eyes. I can't believe how naïve I've been." She was barely in her twenties and her husband was significantly older. She was afraid to leave him.

I started advising her, and at the end of the camping time I felt stronger. Helping another survivor of abuse helped me. I've since learned that helping and encouraging others in similar situations makes survivors grow stronger.

My relationship with my husband continued to deteriorate, and I knew it would never get better. By then I had received a lot of information about sexual abuse from Women in Distress. The most significant thing I learned is that if a wife says no only one time and her husband forces her to have sex, the law says that is rape.

Sometimes I was sick or simply didn't feel like having sex. Many times after fighting during the day, Joel would awaken me in the middle of the night to have sex. I couldn't understand how he could be verbally abusive and only hours later expect me to want to have sex with him.

One morning I told him, "That was abuse last night. And we need to deal with it." I started telling him about the materials and the information I had gotten from the domestic violence center.

Despite his attitude, I made him listen to the truth and showed him pamphlets from Women in Distress. As I should have known, that made him even angrier.

Getting up from the table, he started pacing back and forth. Then he stopped, turned, and stared at me. As he came forward, I knew he was going to hit me. His face flushed and he raised his fist to strike me in the face. I ducked away and said, "I'm sorry. I'm sorry I brought it up; it's not so bad. I don't know what I was thinking." I acted purely on instinct.

"Please, Joel. The kids need to get up and I don't want them to see us fight," I pleaded with him. As a mother, I thought first of the children.

He calmed down and didn't hit me.

Despite my education, appeasing him—taking the blame on myself—seemed to be the only way to bring peace. I had tried to reason with him, which didn't work. I thought of specific instances where God had used people to tell me that it was time to make changes or leave. I held back, denying it was abuse and excusing his behavior.

That morning in 2008 was Diana's first day at a new Christian school.

Although I didn't know it, my daughter had heard the whole fight. After she got to school, she went to her counselor and told her. That same morning the counselor called me. "Your daughter told me that you're an abused wife," the woman said.

"Yes, I am," I said quietly, reluctant to admit it, and the shame overwhelmed me.

"What are you going to do about it?"

"I know I have to do something."

We talked for several minutes and I thanked her for calling. That phone call—my next warning—awakened me once again to the reality: *I am in an abusive situation.* I knew then that God was using my daughter (who I thought was asleep that morning) and her guidance counselor.

That phone call motivated me to take action. *I have to get out of this relationship before he kills me.* I had to figure out how to make the break, but I finally knew I would leave.

I didn't know when or how, but I would leave. That much was settled.

For weeks, however, I held back because I didn't have any money—Joel controlled the finances. Then, the day before I left, I received a check from a credit card company. I had inadvertently overpaid, and they sent me a refund for $2,000. Instead of cashing it, I opened a checking account in my name only.

I had to be careful because Joel kept track of my car mileage. He knew I went to the gym, but I decided not to go that day. A few days earlier my gym trainer, Matt, had suggested a good neighborhood for me to check out. "Go to Coral Springs and look for an apartment."

I was scared but knew I had to take action. I got off at the second highway exit to Coral Springs. Almost immediately, I saw an apartment building with vacancy signs. I went inside and met the manager, was approved, and put down a deposit of $500.

On my first visit to the neighborhood, I was so frightened, I pleaded with God almost constantly to encourage me. That day, I met a woman who lived in the next building. We started talking and I unintentionally opened up to her about my abusive marriage.

"I was in an abusive marriage too," she said. Her two children were the same ages as mine. "I made it. You can make it too."

God used that stranger to give me courage and make me realize that he was at work in my life. I was anxious and worried, and just before we parted I said, "I've never lived alone."

"You'll find a way to survive. And one day you will be happy. You'll see."

I needed to hear those words as well—from someone in the flesh who was not only surviving but thriving.

Not only had I never lived alone, I'd never even had my own bed or bedroom. I was terrified as I moved into an apartment and a strange new world. I didn't have anything, not even a job. I rarely did any work for my realty company, so there was no income from that. Right then I couldn't focus on my lack of money. Instead, I had to trust God and take it one step at a time.

The same day I rented the apartment, I took out a restraining order. Joel's receipt of the restraining order was the beginning of a nightmare for me.

I moved into the apartment with nothing more than my clothes and a few personal items. I had little furniture, and God intervened again. I was able to use a credit card I had received a long time ago but never used. It was such a wonderful experience to buy things that *I* liked.

A man who worked there asked if he could help me, and in our conversation he said he attended Church by the Glades. That morning I had noticed the church, which was across the street from my new apartment. I had asked God to reveal to me if that was to be my new church home.

I thanked God, believing that it was another answer to prayer and an act of grace.

Even with the restraining order, things got worse between us. Joel agreed to let me take clothes and my daughter's furniture from the house. He kept his word but not without a fight. He went to the babysitter and picked up our daughter. I believed he was deliberately being obstinate, as he wouldn't return Diana to me for several days. The restraining order meant that both of us had to appear in court two weeks later.

Living Alone

After having Joel's friends and lawyers convince me not to go through with the restraining order out of fear that my kids would suffer, the day of the court appearance I sat in my car down the street from the court and cried.

Not showing up in court was one of the worst mistakes I ever made. It looked as if I had filed a false restraining order.

One month after our separation, God encouraged me once again—in a different way. My friend from the middle school camp (also a domestic abuse survivor) and I applied for and received scholarships to hear our then-pastor speak at the Billy Graham Conference Center at the Cove in Asheville, North Carolina.

On the trip, the Lord spoke to my heart, saying it was time to start sharing my story about what happened to me when I was growing up in South Florida, especially about the abuse and sex trafficking.

Lord, what if people reject me? What if they tell me what a terrible, worthless person I am? Why would they listen to me? What if they judge me or don't believe me, Lord?

As we drove, I silently argued with God and tried to convince myself that the Lord had not spoken. But God kept pressing on my heart that I was now free from oppression and it was time to start telling everyone my story.

At that conference center, I had a chance to speak for the first time in an environment where I knew I would be safe. I publicly shared my story about my trafficking experiences as a child. To my surprise, people responded warmly and appreciatively. Their acceptance amazed me. But their disbelief that this could happen in America stunned me. Didn't people know how bad society could be to the vulnerable and innocent?

While I was there, God spoke to me again during a worship service: *You are to start an international anti–human trafficking and domestic violence ministry.*

I smile as I think about that. My ministry was born at the Cove just as I was reborn at a Billy Graham crusade when I was twelve years old. It humbled me to think that God would use *my* testimony to help save other twelve-year-olds.

By then I was regularly attending Church by the Glades. On my first day there, a sweet, sensitive man named Cary had taken one look at me and said, "You need divorce care. You're a mess."

Another thing made Church by the Glades special to me. I

had applied for food stamps, and while I waited for approval we had little to eat. My neighbor told me that Church by the Glades gave away free boxes of food and all I had to do was ask. I hadn't done anything like that before, but I was hungry. The experience was humbling. In the past I had usually been the one who gave, and now I found myself to be the one in need.

I went to Church by the Glades and talked to the man who handed out food. He gave me a huge supply. "If you ever need anything," he said, "call Pastor Scott."

The man also gave me Pastor Scott's card, and I talked to him on the phone. If he was going to tell me how wicked I was, I might as well know it now and get it over with. Instead, he listened and advised me to get into a support group. "You need others to stand with you." He prayed with me and was supportive of my action to get out of that abusive relationship.

Ever since my first Sunday at that church, the leaders and members of Church by the Glades have been nothing but supportive to me. I'm grateful to God for their compassion.

———— ☼ ————

One Sunday afternoon, I went to pick up my daughter after a soccer game in Coral Springs. Joel had taken her on Friday and I was supposed to pick her up on Sunday so she could get ready for school the next day here in Broward County. "She has school tomorrow," I reminded him when he said he wanted to keep her.

That began the fighting. He told me she was going home to Miami with him.

We argued, and Joel called the police because he was sure they would let him take her. The patrol car arrived while we were still arguing. Before I could say anything, Joel told the police officer that he was her father and he was taking her to be with his family in Miami for a barbecue.

"No, she has to go with me," I said, "because she has school tomorrow here in Broward. He knows she's supposed to be with me."

In the middle of our argument, I remembered Pastor Scott's card. I took it from my wallet, held it up, and said to the police officer, "I've just started going to this church. He said to call if I needed help."

"Church by the Glades? I know Pastor Scott. He used to be on the police force."

"Really? I didn't know that," I answered. "But he said that if I had any trouble, I should show his card."

"I'm a Christian, and that's where I go to church," the police officer said. "Don't let this man bully you again. And tomorrow you go down to the courthouse and file a restraining order and be sure to put your daughter's name on it, you hear?"

Anger flashed in Joel's eyes, but he said nothing.

Diana went home with me and she was emotionally torn. She loved her father, even if he was abusive.

The next morning after I took Diana to school, I drove directly to the courthouse and filed another restraining order. This time the judge included my daughter in the restraining order. I felt that Joel was using her to get to me. The order wouldn't allow him to see her for two weeks.

The court told me that I could get counseling for the sexual abuse, which I hadn't known. On their advice and that of the Women's Fund in Miami, I went to a place called Broward's Sexual Assault Treatment Center.

After I told them about the abusive situation, they said

they had a month-long waiting list. Then the woman asked me more questions. After I told her everything, she said, "I want you to come in tomorrow. I'll find a way to squeeze you in because you need help *now*."

I felt vindicated because she understood. Even though I had spoken to people for the first time at the Cove, I was now ready to talk about my sexual abuse from childhood and through nearly twenty years of marriage. (I still wasn't ready to talk in depth about my experiences in human trafficking until my very last counseling session. That was how long it took to work through the abuse in my marriage.)

The counselor listened quietly and encouraged me to keep speaking.

"I'm numb and I can't feel my body. It's been like that for at least a year," I said. "I can't feel anything. I'm dying to my sense of self." I was so disgusted with myself that I hated to touch my own body.

She taught me several breathing exercises that helped relax me. I also realized I didn't have to be violated again.

The Sexual Assault Treatment Center helped me, but it still took a year of being away from any kind of sexual abuse before I started to feel my body again or even feel a little healthy.

God brought several wonderful friends into my life, especially women who had experienced abuse and had been in the same financial situation.

To my surprise, my daughter's school counselor helped us. My daughter was still attending the same school, and some of the school staff showed great compassion toward us. My car needed repairs and one of the pastors at my daughter's school, Mark Davis, made sure the church took care of that for me. No one had ever done anything like that before.

I still didn't have a job. I used the financial aid I was receiving from my student loans for our living expenses. I was learning to live on very little. That was how I knew God wanted me to finish my doctoral program. No matter how discouraged I became, God made me know I shouldn't quit school.

For the next two and a half years, I focused on healing and learning to feel again.

Joel and I separated on September 27, 2008, and in February 2009 I filed for support not connected with the divorce. I had hired a lawyer recommended by a family friend. When I approached the office door, the Lord had spoken two words to my heart: *Emancipation Proclamation.*

I was seeking my freedom and that of others to come. After I went to my lawyer's office to discuss filing for divorce, one of the first things he said was, "Whoever files first gets the upper hand."

Having a good lawyer is important, but my lawyer was incompetent. Among many mistakes, he filed the divorce papers in the wrong court. Joel's lawyer sent a female lawyer to convince me that I should drop the divorce petition for the sake of our kids. I believed her, and at nine o'clock that morning I caved in.

Three hours later, Joel and his lawyer filed for divorce in Miami-Dade County. That meant he got there first and had the upper hand. Worse, as part of the divorce petition, Joel asked for me to give him child support, alimony, the house, the business, full custody—everything.

Then to make matters worse, Dad suddenly died of a heart

attack at eighty-seven years old. He had been a millionaire but had spent it all. At the end of his life, Dad died penniless.

——— ☼ ———

Even with all the legal chaos, I knew it was finally going to be over.

At the next court meeting, the judge ordered us to have family counseling, which (as I learned later) he wasn't supposed to do in a case involving domestic violence. However, it turned out to be a good thing.

The counselor held Joel accountable for his actions. "You know this is wrong," she said to Joel. "And even worse, you're putting your daughter in the middle."

At the hearing to make the second restraining order permanent, Joel brought Kipper with him. Only Mom was there for me.

When I saw that he had brought our son, I was hurt and upset, because I think Joel knew I would never say anything about the domestic violence or sexual abuse in our marriage with Kipper present.

When the judge learned that Joel had brought Kipper, he stared at Joel and said, "You are a sick man to bring your son to a restraining order hearing. What kind of parent would do that? Why would you put him through such an ordeal?"

Joel looked down at his feet, but he didn't answer.

"We're not going to have a hearing where kids or family are present," the judge said. "We're not going to bring family members in court to destroy each other." He turned to me and asked, "Have you moved out of the house?"

"Yes, but he's still texting and calling me," I said. "He

harasses me by showing up wherever I am, and he causes problems by trying to intimidate my daughter and me."

The judge turned back to Joel. "You're not allowed to contact her. I mean it. I don't want you to contact her anymore, not by phone or text."

That time Joel listened—I could tell by the expression on his face.

"I'm not going to make the restraining order permanent, because I don't want your son to have to come in here. You have him listed as one of your witnesses and that's ridiculous."

He ordered Joel not to contact me again, and we were finished. I felt relieved and thought of it as a victory.

I was wrong.

My Emancipation Proclamation

Despite all the problems in my life, I was growing stronger. For the past year, I felt as if God had been stretching me, teaching me to stand up for myself, to become assertive and do what I needed to do. But it was extremely difficult.

———☼———

After the worship service on December 6, I went for prayer, and Pastor Mark Davis prayed for me. He offered mentoring and counseling with his wonderful wife, Karen. That was the beginning of a long and fruitful relationship. Pastor Mark made sure that my daughter and I were taken care of.

On December 8, 2010, I was voted in as vice president of a local anti–human trafficking coalition by members of federal and local law enforcement such as the FBI and the Department of Homeland Security. As low as I felt in my personal life, God was building me up in my professional life to be someone I could never have imagined in my wildest dreams.

The worse the divorce process became, the more I yearned to serve God. For me, serving the Lord was the best pain medicine. I was not addicted to anything, so serving him became my way of releasing the pain I felt from my divorce. I asked him to take me anywhere I could serve him; in fact, I said, "Lord, the deeper, the darker, the better."

Christmas came before our final court appearance. Many people were especially kind. Women in Distress gave me gift cards and provided a Christmas tree and presents for Diana and me. About a week before Christmas, a staff member from the church connected to my daughter's school visited and gave me three hundred dollars in gift cards. He told me that it was because the pastor had a heart for single moms and didn't want them to go through Christmas in need. That gesture touched my heart, and I broke into tears.

———— ✦ ————

When we finally went to trial, Joel refused to settle. I think Joel's lawyer insisted on mediation to find out what I wanted before our case was heard. I only got through the mediation because I was taking a class on mediation for my PhD at the time. I could no longer afford a lawyer and had to represent myself in the mediation process. Joel's lawyer argued before the judge that my restraining orders were dismissed because they were false.

"The first one was dismissed because he pressured me not

to show up," I said. "And there had been a temporary restraining order because the judge and I didn't want my son to sit in the court and hear everything."

The judge didn't seem to care about my explanations. That trial lasted nine hours. I had scraped together just enough for a kind Christian lawyer to represent me since I did not qualify for any kind of legal assistance.

We were supposed to have the final divorce hearing and agree on the outcome on January 11, 2011. But Joel's lawyer and the judge had already decided on the dissolution decree weeks before.

My lawyer and I went to the court to attend the final hearing, only to meet Joel and his lawyer and learn what had happened.

"Why did you get a copy and I didn't?" I asked.

The decree had been ordered and signed on December 28, without making my lawyer or me aware so we could be present to hear it.

We learned that the judge had moved to a criminal court and was no longer serving in the family court system. No one had told us in advance. Therefore, there was no need for a hearing—it had already been decided.

The worst part is that the divorce decree said we had joint custody and I had to pay Joel twenty-six dollars a month in child support. "How am I supposed to pay you when I don't even make enough to live on?" I asked him.

He got the house, which would have been impossible for me to keep since I couldn't afford to pay the mortgage. Besides, I wanted my kids to keep their house. Joel also kept the business. Although we shared joint custody of our daughter, who was still a minor, because of school Diana lived with me during the week.

I felt defeated financially, and yet I had the deep-seated assurance that even at that low point God was with me.

I could have fought it, but I didn't. The ordeal had taken two and a half years. But at last, on January 11, 2011, which was also National Human Trafficking Awareness Day, I was finally free.

Free!

A few weeks after that, while getting my tire repaired at Giant Tire through our church's ministry to single parents, I spoke to the owner, Bob, who was a Christian. I mentioned I had gone through a divorce. "We got the papers back, and it's not fair that I have to pay him child support. Most men have to deal with this, not women. Especially not women who have been abuse victims."

"You can file a modification," he said. "It's an amendment to the divorce."

"I can?"

"Why don't you go back over to the courthouse and file one?"

Because I didn't know where to start, I went to the self-help clinic at the court. "How does this process work?" I asked the woman at the desk. "I'm confused."

Patiently, she explained everything. "If you come in with your ex-husband, you don't have to go through another trial.

If the two of you agree, you can go before the judge and he'll sign it without any lawyers present."

"I want to get these twenty-six dollars off the record," I said, almost in tears. "I can't afford to pay him money. Besides that, it's wrong." I was already struggling to make ends meet and had to move out of our comfortable two-bedroom to find something more affordable.

That same day, Dr. Rev. Raul Fernandez-Calienes from the law school told me about a one-bedroom apartment he owned in a quiet, secure neighborhood. When he told me the price, I added and subtracted inside my head and realized that I could figure out how to pay that amount from my school loans. The next day, my daughter and I moved there.

Before long, God did yet another miracle for me.

A few days later, someone knocked on my door.

The man introduced himself and said he was from the bank. "The house is going into foreclosure," he said. The judge had kept my name on the mortgage, so I was also being served.

I didn't want that to happen, so I told him, "I didn't know about this. Give me a few days and I'm sure we can straighten it out."

As soon as he left, I called Joel. "I got the foreclosure papers," I said.

He knew about it, of course, and started to explain.

"I can help you save the house," I said, interrupting him.

"How?"

Instead of a direct answer, I said, "Let's meet at Dunkin' Donuts in twenty minutes."

He agreed.

I was praying and sincerely believed God had guided me to get that self-help packet for an addendum. This time the law would work in my favor.

We sat across from each other, and Joel was obviously ill at ease and angry. For the first time, I knew I could handle his attitude and stay calm.

For several minutes, I let him talk. He explained how and why he didn't pay the mortgage and insisted it was because he had to pay his lawyer, although I felt the real reason was that he didn't want me to keep the house in case it was awarded to me during the divorce.

As soon as he paused, I leaned across the table. "You hurt me a lot through this divorce and in our marriage. But I will help you keep the house if you help me get rid of this erroneous child support."

He didn't answer.

I stared straight at him in a way I'd never done before. "You know what you did to me was wrong. You know you should be paying me child support." I sat there and, instead of being angry, I was filled with compassion for him.

Joel agreed to go to court with me.

His answer shocked me, and at that moment I felt even deeper compassion for him. I was able to look past the pain and say, "I forgive you. I forgive you and I want to help you keep the house for our kids to live in."

Although he wore sunglasses, I could see the tears falling beneath them. Unable to hold back, he started sobbing. He asked why I was being so good to him.

I said, "I forgive you, and we're going to fix it. We'll save the house for you and for the kids. And you know what? I'm not going to dwell on this anymore. I forgive you and God still loves you."

He was amazed at my response, and truthfully, so was I.

I put my hand on his and I prayed for him. That was the beginning of my healing.

Changed

helped Joel save the house from foreclosure. Although he didn't say so, I knew he was grateful.

A week after I told Joel I would help him save the house, we went back to court. On the forms, he filled in low figures until I said, "I handled the accounts for the business. I know how much you and your company make." My voice was surprisingly calm but firm.

He wrote his true income but insisted that I not receive any money from him for child support. He wrote NO CHILD SUPPORT really big across the court documents.

"I'm agreeing to this," I told him, "only because I don't want to have to pay you child support."

———✧———

The woman at the desk, who was either a Christian or an angel, took the forms. She didn't say a word and keyed the information into the computer. When she finished, she looked at him and said matter-of-factly, "You owe her money."

Joel insisted we both had agreed to no child support.

His insistence on no child support was to his detriment when we went before the judge.

A few weeks before we met with the judge, Diana and I moved into our small one-bedroom apartment and started attending St. Andrews Presbyterian Church in Hollywood, Florida. It was close to where we had moved, and I knew several church members there who were wonderful and supportive. I would eventually do my practicum with the Well of Sychar, their Christian domestic violence center.*

A few members of St. Andrews Church met with me for prayer. We pleaded with God for a just judge who would be unbiased and honest.

At court, the judge silently read through the documents. After he finished, the judge looked at Joel. "I understand you want to avoid paying child support?"

I didn't say a word.

My ex-husband insisted that we had an agreement.

"You have no choice. You must pay child support to her." He explained the law of the State of Florida: whichever parent earned more money paid child support.

Joel complained about his having a big mortgage.

"According to the laws of Florida, if you don't pay child

---

*Later, I was the first participant for their Christian domestic violence center, the Well of Sychar. The congregation helped me to start my ministry to girls who came out of trafficking. One of the best things they did was to provide free and safe space for me to meet with those former victims.

support, you will go to jail. You also want me to break the law by agreeing with you?" He paused and then said, "I'm not going to jail for you, and you're not going to avoid paying her child support."

Joel nodded, and I kept quiet.

"And to make sure you pay her, I'm going to tie it to your driver's license. If you choose not to pay through the court, your license will be suspended."

Neither of us spoke to each other until we were out of the courtroom.

God had answered my prayers. I hadn't needed to argue or have a lawyer present. God had been my advocate and judge.

As we walked out of the courthouse, Joel asked if I wanted to have coffee with him. Although shocked, I said, "Yes, I would like to have coffee with you."

By then Joel had calmed down. Instead of just coffee, he treated me to lunch. Although it felt awkward, he was kind and sweet to me. We talked for almost two hours. Even better, we talked in-depth—the way we hadn't opened up to each other in years, if ever.

I could hardly believe we were sitting in a small French café across the street from the Miami-Dade County Courthouse. Especially after we'd just finished our final court hearing and God's hand of mercy had turned events and hearts around.

We both had been humbled by the process of divorce; now we were being real. After years of struggling, everything was in the open, and there was no longer anything to gain or to lose. We were completely honest; it was emotionally exhilarating and overwhelming.

We were able to talk freely, and some healing took place between us, even though it came too late—at the end of a twenty-three-year marriage. I wish we had talked like this years earlier. Because the kids were taken care of and money was no longer an issue between us, we were able to communicate. It wasn't perfect, but it was the best it had ever been. Now I was ready for a wider ministry.

Rescue Ministry

I was asked to volunteer with Shared Hope International's Defenders in conducting truck stop outreaches in Broward County. To do that, we went to major truck depots and made the drivers aware of the danger of minors being sold into prostitution. We helped them understand what kind of suspicious activity to watch for at the places they stop, such as restaurants, gas stations, and motels. We learned how to work with local law enforcement agents.

Of all the outreach work we have done, that is the most dangerous because the pimps are right there with the girls. Those handlers carry weapons and can be unpredictable.

At the invitation of the Secretary of State, George Sheldon, who had been the dean of students when I was at St. Thomas Law School in 2005–2006, I served on the ad hoc Committee for Domestic Minor Sex Trafficking in the State of Florida. Our purpose was to help create a law to protect minors from being criminalized in prostitution and instead to be regarded as victims of human trafficking. We wanted to protect children used as prostitutes and send them to safe environments.

For us to get the law passed, the hardest thing I had to do was to stand before the Florida legislature and law enforcement officials and tell my story. It wasn't easy—it's never easy—but I did it. The same day I stood before them, I also first shared my idea of a faith-based mentoring program from survivors to survivors. That was a big step, and afterward I received the best possible confirmation for emphasizing the faith issue. Several Christians who were in law enforcement heard me speak and they thanked me.

I was part of that committee until it was dissolved by legislation in the summer of 2011. The Safe Harbor Act went into effect January 2013.

No longer are children criminalized as prostitutes here in Florida, because the law now considers them as victims of a crime. This law still needs to make its way to other states throughout the country. Instead of placing children in jail, where many of them had gone previously, the state is supposed to provide funding for safe houses and for professionals to work with those kids who have been identified as trafficking victims.

Statistics show that children who run away from abusive homes are likely to be contacted by a trafficker within twenty-four to forty-eight hours after leaving. I warn children, "Those traffickers won't seem like someone you'll suspect. They'll be kind. Caring. They'll listen and make you feel they want to help you." I end by saying, "Before running away from an abusive situation, first try to get help in finding a safe place to go."

I try to spread the word about our local helpline and the National Human Trafficking Hotline, which is 888-373-7888. If people want to get involved in the fight against human trafficking, they can contact There Is H.O.P.E. For Me, Inc. through our website, www.thereishopeforme.org.

We conduct training and offer free resources on our site, such as a human trafficking assessment tool. This is used by the public school system in Miami-Dade and Broward Counties—as well as by local and federal law enforcement agencies, detention centers, and child protection services—to identify victims of trafficking.

I began sharing my full story within the juvenile jail system in 2010. I also received several invitations to speak at various venues, including juvenile detention centers and public schools. My openness encouraged other girls who had been trafficked to speak out.

One girl explained how she had become a recruiter. One time her pimp took her to a park. He pointed to a nine-year-old girl. "You see that little one? Go get her. We have somebody waiting for her." She recruited the child, and not long afterward she recruited a twelve-year-old girl.

I reported that to law enforcement, and that's what began our unique system of dealing with the trafficking cases that come forward.

Girls tell me horror stories—many of them worse than anything I had endured, such as girls right in the state of Florida who are chained to their beds at night so they can't run away. Their pimps feed them drugs like cocaine to keep them quiet and compliant.

There are different levels of trafficking and different organizations, but they all start by first choosing and then luring vulnerable children. After that, their methods differ. But those organizations are successful because of the *neediness* of their victims.

When I started seeing girls within the juvenile detention facilities coming forward to tell their stories and wanting a safe person to share with, I formed my own organization, There Is H.O.P.E. For Me, Inc. Girls told me they were forced into working without pay as dancers in strip clubs. Many of them told me of being beaten by their pimps.

I had been trained in doing this type of ministry and went into strip clubs to share the gospel message, and I saw many souls saved. I wanted There Is H.O.P.E. For Me, Inc. to be the kind of ministry that went out—like evangelists—to give the Good News and set the captives free, as the Bible declares. We couldn't wait for them to come to us; we had to reach out to them.

This led to starting a ministry in strip clubs. We rely on the Lord to bring gifts of love to us so we can deliver them every month. We also distribute Bibles and have opportunities to share the gospel message.

Many of the dancers in strip clubs are single parents. Most dancers are survivors of some type of abuse. Many live in abusive relationships with boyfriends. Their needs touch me deeply because many of these girls started down the same path I did after being sexually or physically abused as children.

We had to close our office because traffickers found out where we were and tried to infiltrate our organization until their victims came forward. Since we caught on, those former victims are now involved in an investigation.

A church in Coral Springs gave us an office and resource center for the women who come for help. The majority of the girls in the strip clubs aren't trafficking victims but victims of childhood abuse and domestic violence; they're there because they're desperate for work. A few of them broke away from trafficking situations and couldn't get other jobs. Whenever we are faced with young women coming forward, we involve law enforcement. We're bound by a confidential relationship with law enforcement, so we're not allowed to divulge the details.

Most of the trafficking victims in clubs are either American minors or internationals, usually Asian or Russian girls who were brought to the United States under deceptive promises. Once here, they're forced to strip. Their pimps sit in the audience, watch them perform, and wait for them to finish, or they use other girls in the clubs to control them. They maintain such tight control, the girls feel they can't leave. Increasingly, American minors or women being controlled by pimps are being lured into this type of sex trade, and they don't have the opportunity to leave their abusive and exploitative situations either.

Initially, the girls are suspicious when we approach them. We bring them roses, chocolates, pajamas or sleepwear, and New Testaments. We take small gifts to the managers and other employees as well.

If the girls want help, we give them a safe telephone number to call so they can get out and stay out. It doesn't happen frequently, but occasionally a girl who wants to leave that terrible life calls us. Each time we reach out in a safe way and love them. We want them to feel safe by turning to Jesus.

Some of the girls leave stripping because of our involvement, and that's not a problem for the clubs. Unfortunately, there are always plenty of other girls needing jobs and buying into the deceit of the glamour.

———☼———

This kind of ministry brings tremendous highs and lows. When I first began visiting strip clubs, I went as part of a group. One night, eight girls came to the Lord through our efforts. That night God seemed to have infiltrated the whole building with his love. We had gone out to the floor and talked with the manager, and we had the privilege of leading him to Jesus Christ while a girl was dancing. We also gave tracts to most of the customers, and they accepted them. Tears flowed as Jesus broke off the shackles of bondage from all sorts of people, from the managers to the girls and even to some of their clientele.

On the other hand, I've never experienced so much spiritual opposition as I do in that kind of ministry—even more than in the jails or the group homes—and I'm sure it's because we can make such an impact. I say it this way: "If you go into the devil's camp to bring people out to salvation, you'll find opposition—a lot of it—but it's worth the effort."

———☼———

When we first give gifts to the girls, they don't know how to respond. They're used to bargaining and paying for everything. Many take the gifts and then ask, "How much do you want?"

"I don't want any payment," I say and smile. "This is a gift for you."

"You don't want anything?" They don't seem to believe me at first. Why should they? I myself had been enslaved because of such promised kindness, so I understood they were skeptical. Most of the girls in the clubs have a history of abuse and mistrust. Even when they do collect money, those with pimps have to hand over most if not all of it.

"We're here to show you that God loves you," I tell them. "You owe us nothing. *Not ever.* God's love is free for all who want it."

When the dancers want to come out, they need a place to go—and we provide that. We send them to local congregations that collaborate with us, and they provide the girls with food, educate them, and help them find honorable work.

It's surprising to realize who the girls are that end up in strip clubs. One girl in a strip club in Broward had been attending the local Christian school only the year before.

No one is immune.

———— ☼ ————

I remember going into the locker room at the back of one club, and a young girl was sitting with us as we played worship music and ministered to her. She was crying and sucking her thumb. "I don't want to go back out there."

We reach out to those girls and women—and not just to make converts. We talk with them, often play worship music, and do Bible studies right there in the locker room of the club. We show them God's love. God put it in my heart to minister to them with his acts of service. We also pray with the house mothers and managers on a regular basis.

One small act of kindness we perform: we wash their feet. Those young women dance for hours at a time while wearing spike heels, and they need the care we give them. Their feet are sore and bruised. Washing their feet is one of the simplest and kindest things we can do for them. They are grateful because they've known so little true tenderness in their lives.

While we stay in the locker room and minister to a few girls at a time, others are performing out on the floor. We do for them what we can. Many of the performers have issues with church and often feel unwanted or rejected by church members. Drug addiction is common. Several of the women who are struggling addicts are also mothers and have lost their children through the court system.

———— ☼ ————

I worked in a group home for a while when starting my ministry. That was the first time I met children of a girl who worked as a dancer—two boys, and both had been sexually molested because their mom had left them with the wrong people.

I was able to see both sides of that dynamic. The moms cry, "I miss my kids." The children moan, "I wish my mom was here." I've shed many tears over those situations. The case that was the worst for me was a sweet-looking, nine-year-old boy who had to wear diapers. He had been so sexually traumatized, his body would no longer function normally. He finally went to a therapeutic foster home that was equipped to care for him. Such conditions aren't that unusual.

———— ☼ ————

For a long time we ministered without results. When some of the girls finally wanted counseling, they didn't want it at the club. "Where's your place?" they asked. "Where can I come to talk to people? Can you help me?"

That took us to the next step in our growth. Nowadays when we rescue someone out of abuse or sex trafficking, it's a comprehensive process. We offer them not only the firsthand knowledge and experience of a survivor (which *is* the first step), but we also walk them through understanding what they have experienced. Most American trafficking victims don't self-identify as victims of sex trafficking or slavery. They usually see themselves only as victims of abuse, or because of being brainwashed by their pimps, they think they voluntarily do that type of work.

There is so much manipulation involved in human trafficking that it takes time to talk to the girls and boys and get them to trust again. We offer them the opportunity to understand that the front man or woman they have met and perhaps even fallen in love with is just that—a front to a multibillion-dollar-a-year industry. Behind the scenes are rich, older men, many with ties to the Mafia or organized crime.

Once the girls see the truth through a personal example of someone who exited the life, they are much more likely to leave. That's why we have such a high success rate.

———✦———

It wasn't easy to pursue my PhD studies and minister to the girls, who need so much love and time to learn to trust us. Many times I wanted to quit. Yet God continued to encourage me. I wanted to be able to stand before survivors and point out that I dropped out of school in ninth grade but have gone from a GED to earning my PhD.

When I've talked to some of the survivors, they're amazed

and give me exactly the right response: "If you could earn your PhD, there's hope for me." That's what we always say with the ministry. "Because I made it and so have others, why can't you? If there is hope for me, then there is hope for you."

Survivor Stories

Three years after helping to formulate the Safe Harbor Act and using my testimony as a framework, we were able to help rescue seventeen-year-old April out of trafficking—one of the first to benefit from that legislation.

April, who had been victimized several times, now as an adult helps me do training sessions for law enforcement in that same county where she had been trafficked and arrested. No longer the victim, she helped us set free a fifteen-year-old girl, who in turn helped us to set free another fifteen-year-old girl.

From survivors to survivors—it's almost as if we have our own underground freedom railroad out of abuse and human trafficking. I have been called a female Moses because I can help lead them out and help them stay out.

Increasingly, we are experiencing success because we believe we have a mandate from God and we've learned how to help them change. As we work with law enforcement agencies, more and more teens are rescued.

———☼———

April was trafficked in Miami. She came from a single-parent home troubled with addiction and economic disadvantage. Her trafficking started in a convenience store. April was hungry and "a nice man" did a simple thing: he bought her food and was kind to her. That same day, he took her to someone's house to meet a female already caught up in the life. Once there, they tricked her into taking a drug. After she passed out, they locked her inside a room with a padlock on the door. Then her slavery began and they forced her to service many men each night.

April is alive today only because she was able to escape through a bathroom window. She went to jail because she was caught stealing a car. That's where I met her. She had never been reported as a victim of sex trafficking to law enforcement. Worse, it wouldn't be the only time she would be trafficked.

I had to tell April's father because he wouldn't believe her. When he realized that the FBI was involved and that she was cooperating, he finally listened. Because such stories are so horrific, parents don't want to believe them.

April's father isn't alone. I have to inform many parents that their child has been trafficked. Most of them respond with that same disbelieving look and ask, "You mean trafficking happens here?"

"Yes," I tell them, "and your child was a victim of it."

———☼———

In 2013, I drove two girls to Broward College. The first one, Fanny, had come out of a life of prostitution after she had been recruited by an older man. She said she wanted to enroll so she could better her life. Because we were early for her appointment, we sat on a bench and relaxed.

When Fanny answered her cell phone, I paid little attention until I realized that she was being recruited to appear in a porn video.

"Hang up," I said, "and let's talk."

She did, and when she protested that she was no longer in prostitution, I said, "Doing a porn video is the next step, right? And if you take that step, you'll likely be back to the old life."

That day she listened to me and didn't do the porn film. But she might have gone back if I hadn't overheard that conversation. Her mother is dead and she has never had a role model outside of what she learned in our program. I stand in the gap for her—that is, I pray for her and try to be available whenever she needs me. She is now on her way to becoming one of our survivor leaders and life coaches.

——— ☼ ———

Kayla, who had just gotten out of trafficking, was the other girl I took to Broward College. Federal law enforcement had arrested her pimp, convicted him, and taken him out of her life. He was out, but trafficking wasn't. Within weeks, an older man befriended Kayla and persuaded her that she could make a lot of money as a prostitute and retire as a millionaire.

At the college, while Fanny was inside at her appointment, the man drove up and motioned for Kayla to get in his car. I stood in front of the car so he could see that I was there to protect her.

"You can't leave," I told her.

She turned her back on me and started toward the passenger side.

His lure was that he would buy her a new phone. To many that sounds trivial, but although some of the girls may be teens, they still reason like children. The lure of money and material possessions was just too much for her.

"What are you doing?" I asked Kayla. "You just got out of trafficking."

"But he's giving me a new cell phone."

"Are you kidding me? Are you falling for those same old tricks?"

I stood on the road between her and the man in his car and refused to move. "If you take her," I yelled at the man, "I'll call the police! She is underage and you're going to be arrested!"

He put his car into gear and came at me as if he would ram me. I stood in place, hands on my hips, daring him to run me down. When he realized that I wasn't going to move, he threw his car into reverse and turned around. I wasn't able to see his license number.

I wasn't afraid, because I know that God saved me for a purpose. Those traffickers should have killed me when I was thirteen, young, and naïve. Now I'm alive, working for Jesus Christ, and I'm not backing down.

I refused to judge Kayla or give up on her. "I'll always be here for you," I said. "And I won't stop praying for you."

Another survivor I helped was Samantha, who grew up watching her mom and sister engage in prostitution. Samantha refused the advances of her sister's pimps, until one day she was lured to a hotel by a friend and was tricked into prostitution.

Her journey ended when I was introduced to her at Trinity Church in Miami, one of our ministry partners. Through partnership with what I call the underground network of faith-community providers, pregnant Samantha was able to go to a home for unwed mothers.

She found a good job and went back to school. I smile when I think of her, because I had the privilege of being the first person in her life to talk to her about getting out of that life. That same day she accepted Jesus as her Savior.

Mickey, a runaway, was staying with a friend, and one day she went to a Laundromat. While there, a nice-looking, older man came up to her. "You could make money modeling—a lot of money."

Shocked, she stared at him.

"You're beautiful and you're tall," he said. "That's all it takes."

In a soft voice, he praised her good looks and her poise, and he said she had the kind of face cameras love to photograph.

That's all it took to lure the fifteen-year-old runaway. He took her somewhere to teach her about the modeling profession. He showed her pictures of the dead body of another child to scare her into doing what he wanted. Then he threatened to kill her if she didn't do what he wanted. Frightened, she didn't fight him. That same day, he locked her inside a room with an older girl to watch her. Using threats and free cocaine, he turned her into a call girl for him.

After becoming addicted to drugs and being badly beaten, Mickey escaped and went to a medical facility. That's when she told police about the man. Instead of helping her, they arrested her as a criminal because she was a runaway, and they placed her in a juvenile facility. That happened just before the Safe Harbor Act went into effect.

I met Mickey and she listened as I talked to her. Not long after that, she met a number of "boyfriends" who deceived her, and within a short time she went back to drugs and the life of prostitution.

She escaped a second time and contacted me. I helped her report the facts to the police. The trafficker fled and the case is still considered an open investigation.

Mickey is currently out of the life, and I'm still mentoring her. She is now sixteen years old and doing well.

———— ☼ ————

Asha is a lovely blue-eyed, seventeen-year-old blonde. While hitchhiking to see her boyfriend, she accepted a ride from a stranger. He overpowered her, kidnapped her, and forced her to perform sexually for him and his friends.

They learned her father owned a gun, so they told her to get the gun and bring it to them. She made them believe she would, but she never returned.

One day after school she was followed by a man who seemed nice enough. Several times he greeted her, talked nicely to her, and finally made her believe that he had fallen in love with her. He convinced her to go away with him. Once he had her out of the school environment, he gave her alcohol and drugs, and she fell into his trap of using her for prostitution. She never fully knew what she was engaged in until I was called in to work with her by the National Human Trafficking Hotline. Her case manager asked me to help identify her as a victim and work with her from there. She was still in it when I met her. I called in law enforcement, and then they came in and helped her.

When Asha said, "You give me hope," I knew she was on her way to living a normal, healthy life.

On Asha's eighteenth birthday, law enforcement moved her to another state. She emailed that she had seen and shoveled snow for the first time and added, "I feel good about myself."

----- ☼ -----

I met Latoya in a jail facility. She had been recruited out of foster care when she was eleven years old and had been living in human slavery for six years. She was being trafficked by organized crime, and they grossed more than a million dollars a year from the use of her body.

When I met Latoya, she had been rescued by the FBI and placed in jail for her own safety. If she had gone back to her foster home, the FBI said that the Mafia would have killed her. She wasn't in jail because she was a criminal; she wasn't charged with any crime. Instead, she was there because they wanted to keep her safe, and there were very few safe housing options at the time.

Latoya looked like a magazine model. She was tall, thin, and elegant looking. She spoke well and was intelligent. When I began working with Latoya, she didn't want to hear the gospel. All she wanted was to return to her old life.

Shortly after I met her at the jail, she had said, "When I

heard your story I started crying because you talked about organized crime. And that's where I'm at right now. I'm afraid they're going to kill me."

"Those FBI agents are great people," I said, "and they're not going to hurt you. They want to support and protect you the best they can. That's why you're here."

A few minutes later, she said, "You know, Miss Kat, I'm also struggling with going back."

"Why would you want to go back?" I realized I was dealing with the lure of a life that promised money and freedom. I began breaking down the lie that kept pulling her back into that life. "What is it you like about it? Let's talk about that."

"I like the money," Latoya said. "I'm seventeen, and I have my own condo that I share with other girls." It made her feel like a big girl. "Also, I like having nice cars and new clothes when I ride around."

"But is it *your* condo? Is it *your* car? Do *you* get to drive it?" I asked.

"No, somebody else drives us around, and there are always men with us to take care of us and make sure we have everything we need."

"So that's the life. You're making big bucks and you're really somebody. Fancy clothes and all that. Okay, so I know what you like. What don't you like?"

From her answer to the question, I realized she hadn't thought of those issues before. "Well, I don't like when I have my period and I still have to have sex. I don't like it when I have a fever or I'm sick and I'm still forced to have sex. I don't like having sex with men six nights a week."

We talked a little more and she added, "I don't like getting beaten."

"Those sound like pretty good reasons to get away from those people. One other question: What do you think they'll do to you if you come back?"

"I'm not going back!"

Once we worked through her root issues, she came to the conclusion that the life wasn't all it had been made up to be.

"Okay, Latoya, so now that we have gotten to the reality of it, why is it you are still struggling? What is it that would draw you back?"

"I really just want to help my best friend who is still there."

There's always something that pulls at them to come back. No child wants to be sexually abused by multiple partners several nights a week. No child grows up thinking she wants to be in prostitution.

"Good for you. Now let's get the others who are still trapped. But you don't help your friend by going back to that lifestyle. Talk with your law enforcement agents and give them the telephone number for your homegirl, and let them get her out. You don't go back in to get her, because then you'll likely never come out alive."

I tried to speak objectively to her about what it's really like. "You can become somebody and earn money for yourself and not have to earn it doing the things you don't want to do. You don't have to live that kind of life and put up with the abuse and beatings. What if you got AIDS? Would they care? What if you died?"

Latoya started working with law enforcement to bring her friend out. That was the last time I saw her, since federal authorities had to relocate her again for her own safety.

———— ☼ ————

One time, another girl who was sent to recruit a nine-year-old said she had been beaten by her pimp, and twice she was shot—once by a pimp and once by a customer. She badly wanted to get out of that life. And she was willing to cooperate and talk to law enforcement.

But as soon as she got out, an organization I worked with reached out to her—supposedly to help. Instead of seeing the need to connect that child to law enforcement, they exploited her. They did little for her, but they used her story to bring in financial contributions. That experience helped me see the need to start my own program.

The following year, I spoke at another jail and one of the girls recognized me.

"You remember that girl—the one named Natalie—you tried to help?"

"I certainly do. I never heard what happened to her."

"She got out of jail and before long she was back in with the traffickers again."

Tears filled my eyes. That girl had shown such promise.

"Now she's pregnant with her pimp's baby."

Then my tears flowed. That means both parents are now traffickers. That sweet girl, whom I met when she was seventeen, is now an adult and they have a baby together, and both of them recruit children for the life of sex slavery.

Those children have become the next level of our society in normalizing prostitution and human trafficking in the home by both parents, and it will continue to get worse unless we stop the business of trafficking.

The saddest fact for me isn't just those like April, Fanny, Samantha, Mickey, Asha, Latoya, Natalie, and me who were lured into the trade. Some addicts sell their children to feed their drug habit, and they normalize prostitution as a way of life here in the United States.

It may be impossible to achieve, but our purpose is to stop trafficking in our lifetime through the voices of survivors helping other survivors. As survivors are empowered and healed, they find a purpose for living.

We do our ministry on a biblical basis. We want to give hope to those who are enslaved. Alone, I may only be one survivor, but united we are stronger than all of the traffickers. Together we can stop human trafficking!

As I give of myself and reach out, I clearly remember Billy Graham pointing at me. "Remember this: God will never leave you or forsake you."

And he never has.

If there is hope for me, then there *is* hope for you and for everyone.

Setting the Captives Free

Today traffickers are using new methods to recruit, especially the internet, including sites such as Facebook, BlackPlanet, Mocospace, Backpage, and SugarDaddie. Traffickers use these websites to secretly buy and sell children. One of the initiatives that we've taken from the Thorn Foundation is to do a follow-up survey with our clients. When we come into contact with exploited children or they come to us, we have them fill out information and we help make sure that the kids are placed in an emotionally safe environment.

Experts are delighted with the work we're doing to weed out those traffickers, because they know we have direct access to survivors of trafficking. The National Human Trafficking Hotline in Washington, DC, works with us.

In our program, as soon as girls come forward we connect them with law enforcement. Many of the girls we've helped rescue have worked with law enforcement and we've seen successful prosecutions of their traffickers, some facing nearly a life sentence in prison while others were deported. As a survivor, I believe we need to help the girls, and the only way to stop trafficking is to shut down the traffickers.

Another organization called GEMS (Girls Empowering Mentoring Services), based in New York, mentors girls to help them stay out of the life by providing exit strategies and support. Rachel Lloyd, a woman from England who is also a survivor, founded the GEMS program in the United States. When I first began doing street outreach in 2009, I worked with several of her people, and now I myself have been trained under her tutelage.

We want to be led by God's Spirit; therefore, we don't beg or try to force people to leave their lifestyle. We want them to know about honor, dignity, respect, and love for themselves and for others. For them to embrace such qualities, we have to model it ourselves.

We also try to do special things for survivors. For example, in August 2012 we took a group of our rescued survivors on a retreat to the Ritz-Carlton Hotel in Naples, Florida, and we took others to Disney World in Orlando. Now we have our first group of Survivor Leaders, whom we are training to be good listeners to others coming out of the sex trade. This group of survivors we have helped rescue are now our leaders, listeners, and mentors to those in the public school system and universities who need to talk to a healed survivor.

We have to convince the girls that there are people like us who care and who stand behind them. If we, God's people, don't stand up for them, who will? If we're not there to guide them, most of them will go back into the old lifestyle. But because we speak to them from the honest example of volunteers and an army of survivors who have successfully come out of that life, many of them want to be free.

Pulling them out of the lifestyle is hard enough, but that's only the beginning. I point that out because a number of churches and organizations are zealous to free the girls but don't stay with them and help them adjust to a new life. Those girls have been damaged emotionally and often physically. It's not easy for them to make that adjustment. Because they've encountered so little integrity, they don't know how to trust honesty. Not only do we have to prove we love them, we also have to prove ourselves to them—many, many times. But it's worth the effort to see the miracles God does in their lives.

Part of what drives me is remembering my own life. If someone had given me support or helped my mother when she was living in an abusive marriage, my life might have been different. For me, the one thing that kept me going in spite of all the abuse was that I knew God loved me and I knew my mom loved me. If these children have just one safe person whom they can trust, they will be able to move beyond their past.

That probably sounds odd to some, because I was weak, terrified, and had no one in whom I could confide. Yet God was lovingly patient with me even though I failed hundreds of times. And he has given me the privilege of leading many trafficking survivors to a personal relationship with Jesus Christ.

Not many of those survivors knew—truly knew—the God who loves them. We try to model that for them. We've helped a number of survivors by going into a support ministry with them. We constantly say, "You can do this, you know."

Instead of saying, "Oh, you poor victim," we say, "You are more than a conqueror through Christ who gives you strength, and through him you can do all things!" We never give up on them, no matter what!

Not only is hope the concept of our ministry, it's also an acronym.

H = Healing
O = Opportunity
P = Purpose
E = Empowerment

God has used everything that I've gone through to help those kids and young women. There aren't many experiences the girls talk about that I can't identify with. I hate what happened to me, but part of my redemption is to see God taking my pain, turning it around, and using it to help others who are where I once was.

After someone comes out of the sex trade, we refer them for services such as free tutoring, counseling, food, and clothing through like-minded individuals, faith-based organizations, or churches that have agreed to our antiviolence and traffic-free standards. Through the kindness of Christian congregations, we offer free Bibles and study guides. We're trying to help survivors grab hold of their identity in Christ and gain a vision for their future. Then they too can live victoriously.

I also created a human trafficking assessment tool that is being used nationwide within the public school and foster care systems and by law enforcement to help identify those who might become or have been victims of trafficking. We know, for instance, that if children come from economically disadvantaged backgrounds with abuse in their past, have prior exposure to drugs or alcohol, or if their parents have been in any form of prostitution or commercial sex, those factors predispose children to the vulnerability of being trafficked.

Even though not everyone is vulnerable to being picked up by traffickers, kidnapped, lured, manipulated, or taken, we need to be aware of the factors that exist and protect the innocent and susceptible. Traffickers lurk everywhere. They go into the malls, they sit in McDonald's, they infiltrate our school systems, and they take their kids to the park and to hotel pools.

The Trafficking Victim's Protection Act—a law that protects victims and governs anti-trafficking in the United States—says that anyone engaged in any form of paid sex who is under the age of eighteen is automatically a victim of trafficking. If anyone gains financially through the use of a child's body for commercial sex, that law says the child is a victim of human trafficking and that the trafficker has committed a federal crime, whether they're a parent, boyfriend, false friend, or child protection worker.

In the fall semester of 2012, when I first began to work on this book, we uncovered *sixteen* children in three schools—one middle school and two high schools—in the southern region of America. They were being recruited right at their schools, on Facebook, through friends, and even through school computers that they were using to communicate with their pimps.

Through many methods, kids are seduced into trafficking. It often begins with posing for pictures or videos. They start taking off an item or two of their clothing, and it seems harmless. Each time they take off a little more until they're involved in compromising sexual acts that they never thought they would be involved in. Then they're ashamed and feel worthless for being tricked into that life—which makes them easy targets for total manipulation and domination. By posting compromising photos online, children are letting traffickers know that they are easy targets for recruitment into false modeling scams, abusive boyfriends, or false-friend scenarios.

———☼———

Let's look at the money. At the time of this writing, a sex act with a child costs on average $160 to $180, with the trafficker usually getting paid $50 to $100. Payment to the recruiter (usually an older child) takes another $20 to $30. Payment to the hotel runs $30 to $50. Girls like April, who we rescued in Miami, end up with maybe twenty bucks. It's not unusual for those girls to service ten men in a single night, but that depends how deeply into the life they are. Usually it's only one man in the beginning. Then two a night. Then three. Too often, a middle schooler who earns $200 a day thinks she's hit the jackpot.

One child can bring traffickers up to $3,000 a night. And how many times a year does that child have to perform? One child who was rescued said she had to perform six nights a week, 52 weeks a year. That's almost a million dollars a year, and she was only *one* of their exploited children. Do you know how much sexual abuse that child had to endure for traffickers to make that much money?

Once victims become desensitized, they do what becomes familiar. They stop struggling and move into a variety of normalizing and numbing coping mechanisms to alleviate the reality of constant sexual abuse. These experiences often open the door to domestic violence as victims accept this as a way of life. And worse, they think that's normal. My PhD dissertation, *Vulnerability Factors, Lures, and Recruitment Methods Used to Entrap American Children into Sex Trafficking,* shows the results of trafficking on American children and how they develop certain coping mechanisms to deal with these effects.

Who knows this better than I do?

Drugs play a major role. If children become addicted, they are more likely to be exposed to trafficking to pay for those drugs. I tell kids, "You can't control what happens to you after you open the door to drugs. Just say no to drugs!" They don't realize how much worse their lives can become once they start using drugs. They could be locked inside a room, kept prisoner in a brothel, or chained to a bed. And that's not just in the movies; it's reality for many victims.

Because I help bring the children out, I follow through with law enforcement, social services, and churches. To do that usually means sooner or later I have to talk with the child's parent. When I meet with parents at a school or facility, I have to say, "Your child has been a victim of a crime. Please work with us in helping them to get those bad people out of their lives."

Our girls who have cooperated with law enforcement have never had to go to trial. We have created collaboration efforts with a unique process to make sure that trafficking is stopped *and* that the first time a girl comes forward becomes an empowering time to the survivor. The girls who are involved have gained from working with law enforcement and are free to assist when they see that they are actually helping others get out or preventing trafficking from happening to somebody else.

I'm not part of a law enforcement agency, but I work alongside such agencies to end trafficking. Many agencies are now training their personnel to become victim-centered and are compassionate and help the survivors of this crime find strength.

"Be a safe person" is the first thing I tell adults who want to help at-risk children. Become the person to whom they can turn. If you feel inadequate to help, say so and give them a list of individuals and organizations that care.

Those exploited children also need to know they can tell what happened to them. They need to speak up and be heard. They need a voice—a voice for the voiceless in our society.

Once the kids we work with decide to come out of trafficking, we take them to church. The majority of them turn to Jesus Christ for salvation and hope. We're excited because several survivors have been baptized and are becoming involved in a local church.

Others, obviously, are still in the seeking process, but so far we have a high success rate where kids don't return to that life. They're less likely to go back if people like us can help them break that invisible bondage and provide a mentoring relationship with a safe, Christian adult. Those children can finally realize that they are loved and lovable and that someone really does care about them.

We work with the parents and try to provide parent-like ministry. We cooperate with other groups and local congregations to provide free parenting classes. Those within law enforcement have asked us to form parenting support groups, because the parents of these children also need support.

One thing that makes our ministry unique is that it is *from* survivors *to* survivors of human trafficking, domestic violence, and other sexual exploitation. If you want to help, consider partnering with a survivor-based organization. Those who are being trafficked will more likely identify with a survivor of trafficking or abuse.

Even once they're free, survivors have many, many aftereffects. Some of them deal with serious mental health issues, such as post-traumatic stress disorder and bipolar disorder. With no one around them to care for their well-being, some deal with financial issues, homelessness, loss of identity, and feelings of not belonging. Others—both boys and girls—struggle with bisexuality and homosexuality, and we want to be there to encourage and not judge them. It's easier for some of them to return to the streets or to traffickers if they're not provided with a safe mentor or homelike environment where they can be nurtured and feel supported.

— ☼ —

From darkness into light. That is the life we offer them, and we work with others to see it through to the end. This is a place of spiritual battle for those victimized children. We rejoice when girls and boys come out of human trafficking. The ones who have come out of that life help us mentor the younger ones. I give those young people the same message I received and embraced. *Remember this: God will never leave you or forsake you.*

If you have been a victim of human trafficking or any form of sexual exploitation or domestic violence, I want to hear from you.

Please contact There Is H.O.P.E For Me, Inc. via our website, www.thereishopeforme.org, or email me at info@there ishopeforme.org.

About There Is H.O.P.E.
For Me, Inc.

Our purpose is to rescue and restore victims of abuse and human trafficking. That is, we specifically help to identify children and adults who have not been previously identified by law enforcement as survivors of human trafficking and abuse. We seek to help those who are caught up in the life and are victims of abuse or domestic minor sex trafficking. We do whatever we can to rescue them through our unique faith-based rescue and restoration program.

We use a Christian-based, life coaching program from the American Association of Christian Counselors for helping survivors of human trafficking and abuse. We help them rebuild their lives by referring them to other safe, faith-based programs. We strengthen and encourage survivors to help rescue others.

If your church wants to start such a ministry:

1. Our ministry is *from* survivors *to* survivors. If you want to help, consider partnering with a survivor-based organization. Those who have been trafficked will more likely identify with a trafficking or abuse survivor. No voice is as powerful as those who have been inside human trafficking.

2. Learn everything you can about reaching out to victims. Don't start a ministry without prayer and study.

3. Work with survivor groups. There Is H.O.P.E. For Me, Inc. has survivors nationwide whom we connect with on a regular basis. A bad or ineffective organization can be worse than no organization, because such groups fail to encourage victims to come out. They may exploit survivors for their own gain, and in so doing, they revictimize them.

4. Currently, we are developing a manual on how to identify trafficking victims and develop a survivor-based anti–human trafficking ministry. Go to our website, www.thereishopeforme.org, and use our free tools. We also have a section called Additional Resources. Avail yourself of them.

5. Even if you don't become a direct advocate for those children, support advocates in prayer. Encourage those who reach out. As you are able, support them with your money. You can donate clothes, food, personal items, or professional services. Retirees, especially former teachers, have so much to offer survivors, and our kids especially need their love.

6. Most of all, ours is a love ministry. We never give up on our survivors. They need to know they're important and worthwhile. No judgment. Lots of love and great patience. Too often their parents were so busy they didn't make time for them, or their families were dysfunctional.

Many of those children and young people have never known a healthy adult. *You might be the first healthy adult to whom they can relate.*

More than once I've had to stand between a girl and a trafficker. Or between a girl and a john. I will stand in the gap for them. Will you?

Acknowledgments

This is my "life verse" through which the Holy Spirit constantly encourages me in reaching out to those who are suffering:

> The Spirit of . . . the LORD has anointed me
>   to proclaim good news to the poor.
> He has sent me to bind up the brokenhearted,
>   to proclaim freedom for the captives
> and release from darkness for the prisoners.
> (Isaiah 61:1)

I thank God for all the individuals, churches, and organizations that helped me along the way. Together we are rescuing one life at a time. Most of all, I'm grateful to my Lord and Savior Jesus Christ, God the Father, and his precious Holy Spirit who leads and guides me daily into all my activities.

I want to give special thanks to:

- My mother, Ella, who always loved me and never gave up on me. And because of her love and example, we never give up on our girls here either.
- My brother, Daniel, who has been a source of strength to me.
- My daughter, Diana, who has been and is my inspiration.
- My son, Kipper, whom God used to bring me back to himself.
- My wonderful coauthor and teacher, Cecil Murphey, without whom this book would not be possible. His consistent love and care for me and my family have truly made a difference in my life and now in the lives of many other survivors through the use of this book and more to come.
- Billy Graham, for leading me to my wonderful Savior, my first love, the Lord Jesus Christ.
- Deidre Knight, our literary agent, and Vicki Crumpton, our editor. Both have been so encouraging to me.
- Steve Lawson, for making all this possible by connecting me with Cecil.
- To all of the wonderful participants in our program, There Is H.O.P.E. For Me, Inc., who have overcome so much—this book is for you.
- My wonderful mentors and supporters who have traveled this road with me and helped and encouraged me so much along the way: Dr. Siegfried Wiessner, Dr. Roza Pati, and Dr. Rev. Raul Fernandez-Calienes from St. Thomas University School of Law in Miami. Your tireless and consistent encouragements have helped more than you can imagine. St. Thomas was the place where I learned and experienced that I had the right to dignity and respect. My speaking and writing career began there.

- David Batstone, founder of Not For Sale, who inspired me through his book *Not for Sale*.
- Rachel Lloyd, Girls Empowering Mentoring Services, NY, for helping and now mentoring me along the way into survivor leadership.
- Women in Distress of Broward County.
- The Heath Evans Foundation.
- Marti Wibbles, Palm Beach Counseling.
- Dr. Dustin Berna, my PhD committee chair; my committee members, Dr. Lenore Walker and Dr. Robin Cooper; and many Nova Southeastern University professors without whom my PhD and academic learning in excellence would not have been possible.
- Carmen Pino, Supervisory Agent in Charge, Department of Homeland Security.
- Alan Santiago and Jose Olivera, Supervisory Special Agents, Federal Bureau of Investigation, without whom I would not have been given an opportunity to see how beneficial law enforcement could be.
- Trinity International University, South Florida Campus.
- The people of St. Andrews Presbyterian Church, Hollywood, Florida, who loved me when I needed it most.
- I am grateful to my sisters in Christ who have suffered before me in domestic violence but lovingly cared enough to show me the way out.
- To all There Is H.O.P.E. For Me, Inc. board members, past and present, and our many volunteers, donors, and supporters who encouraged me and my work all along the way.
- To my many friends, spiritual leaders, and encouragers: thank you. Without you, many times I would have fallen into despair.

Katariina Rosenblatt, PhD, is living proof of the promise she heard long ago at a Billy Graham crusade that God would never forsake her. Katariina has a PhD in conflict analysis and resolution and works closely with law enforcement agencies such as the FBI and Homeland Security to eliminate human slavery. She also founded There Is Hope For Me, Inc., a nonprofit organization dedicated to freeing other victims of human trafficking. She has been featured on CNN and in *Today's Christian Woman* and lives in Florida.

Cecil Murphey has written or coauthored more than 130 books, including the bestselling *90 Minutes in Heaven* with Don Piper and the autobiography of Franklin Graham, *Rebel with a Cause.* He was a collaborator on the bestseller *Gifted Hands* with Dr. Ben Carson. Cecil resides in Georgia.

there is HOPE *for me*

There Is **H.O.P.E.** for Me, Inc. reaches out to help survivors of domestic violence and human trafficking. The main purpose of this organization is to conduct outreach to and be a resource for survivors and their families. Help is needed to end human trafficking, and we can all do our part. Our part here is to help by providing Healing, Opportunity, Purpose, and Empowerment to survivors of these crimes.

Visit **TherelsHopeforMe.org** to Learn More

"A searingly honest story of one woman's awakening from a coma after her baby's birth—and her long road back. . . . *Unforgettable.*"

—ERIC METAXAS, *New York Times* bestselling author

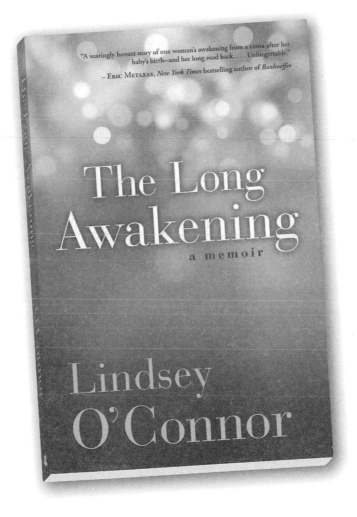

"May this story bring hope to anyone who has suffered tragedy. There is life after loss. It comes after a monsoon of tears. **But it comes.**"

—from the foreword by **Max Lucado**